AF572358

Architecture in Color Drawings

Other McGraw-Hill Books by John S. M. Chen

Architecture in Pen and Ink

Architectural Perspective Grids: Three-Dimensional Design and Perspective Construction Simplified with William T. Cooper, AIA

Architecture in Color Drawings

John S. M. Chen, AIA

McGraw-Hill

New York San Francisco Washington, D.C. Auckland Bogotá
Caracas Lisbon London Madrid Mexico City Milan
Montreal New Delhi San Juan Singapore
Sydney Tokyo Toronto

Library of Congress Cataloging-in-Publication Data

Chen, John S. M.
Architecture in color drawings / John S. M. Chen.
p. cm.
ISBN 0-07-011405-6 (hardcover)
1. Architectural drawing—Technique. 2. Color drawing.
I. Title.
NA2726.2.C54 1996
720′.22′2—dc20 96-28027
CIP

McGraw-Hill
A Division of The McGraw-Hill Companies

1 2 3 4 5 6 7 8 9 0 1IMP/1IMP 9 0 1 0 9 8 7 6

ISBN 0-07-011405-6

The sponsoring editor for this book was Wendy Lochner, the editing supervisor was Jane Palmieri, and the production supervisor was Donald Schmidt. It was set in Palatino by Renee Lipton of McGraw-Hill's Professional Book Group composition unit.

This book was printed and bound in Hong Kong through Print Vision, Portland, Oregon.

Contents

Introduction	vii
Acknowledgments	ix
1. Study Drawings in Color	**1**
Drawings by Cesar Pelli	2–7
Drawings by Tadao Ando (Japan)	8–12
Drawings by Charles Gwathmey	13–14
Drawings by Eric Owen Moss	15
Drawings by Robert Venturi	16–19
Drawings by Sir Norman Foster (England)	20–22
Drawings by John Chen	23–28
Drawings by Maynard M. Ball	29–30
Drawings by Helmut Jahn	31–41
Drawings by Yi Gang Peng (China)	42–43
Drawings by Arthur Cotton Moore	44–46
Drawings by Antoine Predock	47–49
Drawings by Ricardo Legorreta and Armando Chavez (Mexico)	50–51
Drawings by Willem van den Hoed (The Netherlands)	52–53
2. Field Drawings in Color	**55**
Drawings by Paul Stevenson Oles	56–58
Drawings by Gilbert Gorski	59–62
Drawing by Thomas Schaller	63
Drawings by Antoine Predock	64–66
Drawings by Richard Fitzhugh	67–79
Drawing by Maynard M. Ball	79
Drawing by Peter Edgeley (Australia)	80
Drawings by Albert Handell	81–91
Drawings by Ying Tian Liang (China)	92–93
Drawings by Joe Mayer	94–99
Drawings by Sergei Tchoban (Germany)	100
3. Presentation Drawings in Color	**101**
Drawing by Venturi, Scott Brown and Associates, Inc.	102
Drawings by Richard Meier & Partners Architects	103–104
Drawings by Arthur Erickson Architectural Corporation (Canada)	105–110
Drawing by John Stuart Pryce	111
Drawings by Howard Associates	112–116
Drawings by Paul Stevenson Oles	117–118
Drawings by Sergei Tchoban (Germany)	119–121
Drawings by Gilbert Gorski	121–133
Drawing by Ying Tian Liang (China)	134
Drawings by John Chen	135–140
Drawings by Thomas Schaller	141–143
Drawings by Richard Fitzhugh	144–147
Drawing by M. Saleh Uddin	148
4. Pen and Ink Drawings with Color	**149**
Drawings by Rael D. Slutsky	150–155
Drawings by Manuel Avila	155–164

Drawings by Howard Associates 165–169
Drawing by Yi Gang Peng (China) 170

5. Time-Saving Color Drawings **171**

Drawings by John Chen 172–182
Drawings by Gene Streett 183–184
Drawing by Christopher Grubbs 185
Drawings by Peter Edgeley (Australia) 186–191
Drawing by Richard Fitzhugh 192
Drawing by Arquitectonica 193

6. Electronic Drawings in Color **195**

Drawings by View By View Inc. 196–201
Drawings by Paul Stevenson Oles/Advanced Media Design Inc. 202–205
Drawings by John Hawkins 206–209
Drawings by Thomas Singer 210–211
Drawing by Howard Associates 212
Drawings by Haigo Shen & Associates, Architects and Engineers (Taiwan) 213–217
Drawings by Ken Yeang (Malaysia) 218–219

Introduction

In Genesis 9:16-17, God said, "Whenever the rainbow appears in the clouds, I will see it and remember the everlasting covenant between God and all living creatures of every kind on the earth. This is the sign of the covenant I have established between me and all life on the earth." The rainbow is a display of multiple colors. God created colors and also created light so people can see the colors. Color enriches the lives of people and makes all creatures more pretty and things more enjoyable. Le Corbusier once said: "Here is the golden rule...With color you accentuate, you classify, you disentangle. With black and white you get stuck in the mud and you are lost. Always say to yourself: Drawings must be easy to read. Color will come to your rescue." The advantage of color drawing compared to black-and-white drawing is that it depicts the architect's design concept better. It also adds another dimension of value and lets the viewer enjoy the richness of the design project and its relationship with the environment.

During my college years, we were trained to a style of architectural rendering pertaining to the techniques developed by the École des Beaux Arts. I still believe this strict, essential, but sometimes excessive, training is a missing link in today's architectural education. However, technology has changed tremendously since that time. The word "rendering" itself often gives people an impression that it is an act done slowly and repetitively. This is no more the case with today's technology.

Atop all changes is the computer revolution. Not only can the computer draw precise construction drawings, it also can draw multiple three-dimensional drawings in a fraction of the time such work used to require. Not only can these three-dimensional drawings be in skeleton forms called "wireframes," they can also be in finished color renderings, even in animation. With all these things happening, architects are starting to give second thoughts to the process of design. The traditional way is to start a project from floor plan to elevations and sections (so called two-dimensional design) most probably in black and white, and to use three-dimensional drawings only occasionally in the final moment. With electronic technology, architects can jump right into three-dimensional design and right into colors. The concept and method of three-dimensional design were discussed in my previous book, *Architectural Perspective Grids: Three-Dimensional Design and Perspective Construction Simplified* (McGraw-Hill, 1995).

In three-dimensional design, the perspective/color drawing is not just an end product, but the lifeline that links the whole process of design. The computer application together with the everchanging new graphic equipment and products (such as airbrush equipment, new pens, markers, felt pens, color pencils, new papers) made color drawings much easier. More and more architects are applying color to the very early stages of their design in order to communicate better with their client and even themselves. These color study drawings are seldom seen in other architectural color drawing books.

Color field drawings are also often ignored. These color field drawings do not bring an immediate economic benefit to the architect or artist. Many do these drawings just for the pleasure. Some draw them to create a mood or a certain atmosphere. However these drawings will later play an important role in the creativity and improving the graphic skills of the architect or artist and help them to understand what role color, texture, time, and motion play in architecture.

Color pen and ink drawing has the advantage of producing color drawings and black-and-white versions of these drawings at the same time, and can be used for different purposes.

To expedite and improve the slow and arduous process of traditional methods of "rendering," many architects and illustrators are ingeniously using the newly developed technologies and available new graphic products to create shortcuts and artifices that drastically reduce time and labor, and develop time-saving architectural presentation techniques.

Due to the limited space of a conventional printed book, it is impossible to include all the "how-to's" of design communication in this confined space. This is a portfolio of the work of those famous in the field—their magnificent drawings are a feast for your eyes, and their updated techniques will be a unique inspiration for architects, city planners, landscape architects, professors, researchers, illustrators, and students of environmental design.

John S. M. Chen

Acknowledgments

Without the contributions of architects, illustrators, and academicians in the United States and around the world, this book would not be a reality. Special appreciation must be given to foreign contributors; due to their contributions and those of many American firms dealing with international projects, it is possible for this book to include drawings of projects and buildings from Australia, Austria, Bangladesh, China, Cuba, the Czech Republic, England, France, Germany, Iraq, Italy, Japan, Korea, Kuwait, Lebanon, Malaysia, Mexico, The Netherlands, Nicaragua, Poland, Russia, Saudi Arabia, Scotland, Senegal, Singapore, Spain, Taiwan, Thailand, Turkey, the United Arab Emirates, and other countries.

I am grateful to former Senior Editor Joel Stein and the present Senior Editor Wendy Lochner of McGraw-Hill Professional Book Group, who shared my idea to put this color architectural drawing book together and to include the latest developments in the field. I would also like to thank those architects and their staff members at the offices of Arthur Erickson, Sir Norman Foster, Helmut Jahn, Richard Meier, Arthur Cotton Moore, Cesar Pelli, Antoine Predock, Haigo Shen, and Robert Venturi who gave their precious time to discuss the role of color drawings in their work.

I would like to express my gratitude to Harry Robinson III, FAIA, Interim Vice President of Howard University, who supported and backed my initial idea. I am indebted to Victor Dzidzienyo, Dean of the School of Architecture and Planning, as well as Associate Dean Kathryn Prigmore, who gave continuous support for the book. I must also thank Professor José Mapily and Mr. Peter Edgeley, who shared their knowledge on time-saving architectural presentation techniques, Mr. Dick Howard on formal renderings, Mr. Mieczylaw Boryslawski and Mr. Richard Dubrow on computer renderings, Mr. Rael Slutsky and Mr. Manuel Avila on color pen and ink drawings, Mr. Richard Fitzhugh and Mr. Albert Handell on color field sketches, and Professor Daniel Herbert on study drawings.

I would like to express special appreciation to Miss Ruth Huang, who helped me to organize and edit the book. Her diligent, meticulous work expedited the completion of the manuscript. My gratitude also extends to my wife Hui Fang Mai Chen. Without her patience and understanding, the long and strenuous effort to complete this project would not have been possible. I dedicate this book to her.

Chapter 1

Study Drawings in Color

Study drawings are the very first sketches or drawings the architect does for his/her project. Sometimes the study drawing may be a recording of an instant inspiration—a thought the architect has in mind that transfers to his/her hands and draws out the image. Not all images are of building/buildings; they may be diagrams showing the layout of spaces or the exploration of ideas. Although the majority of design drawings are rough and loose, most probably in freehand, showing the incompleteness and the continuity of the design, on other occasions when the architect wants to make a strong statement of his/her concept, these drawings can also be in hardline or somehow more rendered. That is why I'm reluctant to use the word "sketch" to cover all aspects of study drawings.

A definition of study drawings is given in Daniel M. Herbert's book, *Architectural Study Drawings:* "They are the designer's principal means of thinking: the origin, nature, and methods of obtaining knowledge in architectural design can be explained largely in terms of a few culture-dependent properties of study drawings" (Van Nostrand Reinhold, New York, 1993).

Adding color to study drawings makes the designer's concept more understandable and more convincing. When color is used, the meaning of the design becomes obvious, thus creating an atmosphere to celebrate the design environment. When I interviewed Cesar Pelli on his pastel drawings for the Petronas Towers in Kuala Lumpur, he said he drew them for his own pleasure and "searching images of something that echoes within oneself." He was fascinated with the constantly changing tropical sky and wanted to create a symbolic gateway—a passage towards that sky. Pages 2–4 are a series of these drawings and the rendering on the right of page 4 is the final image of this pair of the world's tallest buildings (until the time of this writing). I cannot imagine how Mr. Pelli's message could be conveyed if colors were not used in his drawings.

Colors in study drawings do not necessarily represent the actual colors of the design. Some are used to emphasize certain issues in the design, others are used for color coding or for ambience. Many architects use only a single color or a few colors in their study drawings, thus creating the individual characters of these architects' styles.

The individuality of the architects' styles is not only represented in what or how many colors they use, but also depends on the intensity of these drawings and the media used. Whether they are the fluid black and red lines used by Eric Owen Moss, the fussy yet dynamic and meaningful drawings of Sir Norman Foster, the colored ink drawings by Helmut Jahn drawn with several Mont Blanc or Porsche fountain pens, the formal pencil on lithograph print by Tadao Ando or the more rendered drawings by Arthur Cotton Moore, they are the signatures of these architects. I can see no other drawings, except these study drawings, that can represent the character and the style of these architects: the way they think and the way they explore the design issues.

CESAR PELLI: Sketches of Petronas Towers, Kuala Lumpur, Malaysia. *Oil pastels on vellum.* [*© Cesar Pelli & Associates 1994. All rights reserved.*]

CESAR PELLI: Sketches of Petronas Towers, Kuala Lumpur, Malaysia. *Oil pastels on vellum.* [*© Cesar Pelli & Associates 1994. All rights reserved.*]

CESAR PELLI: Sketch of Petronas Towers, Kuala Lumpur, Malaysia. *Oil pastels on vellum.* [*© Cesar Pelli & Associates 1994. All rights reserved.*]

CESAR PELLI & ASSOCIATES: Petronas Towers, Kuala Lumpur, Malaysia. Renderer: Lee Dunnette. *Airbrush acrylic on photo paper.* [*© Cesar Pelli & Associates 1993. All rights reserved.*]

CESAR PELLI: Sketches of the North Terminal, Washington National Airport, Washington, D.C. *Oil pastels on vellum.* [*© Cesar Pelli & Associates 1994. All rights reserved.*]

CESAR PELLI: Sketch of a private residence in the West, Wyoming. *Oil pastels on vellum.* [*© Cesar Pelli & Associates 1991. All rights reserved.*]

CESAR PELLI: Sketch of a resort hotel, Fukuoka, Japan. *Oil pastels on vellum.* [*© Cesar Pelli & Associates 1994. All rights reserved.*]

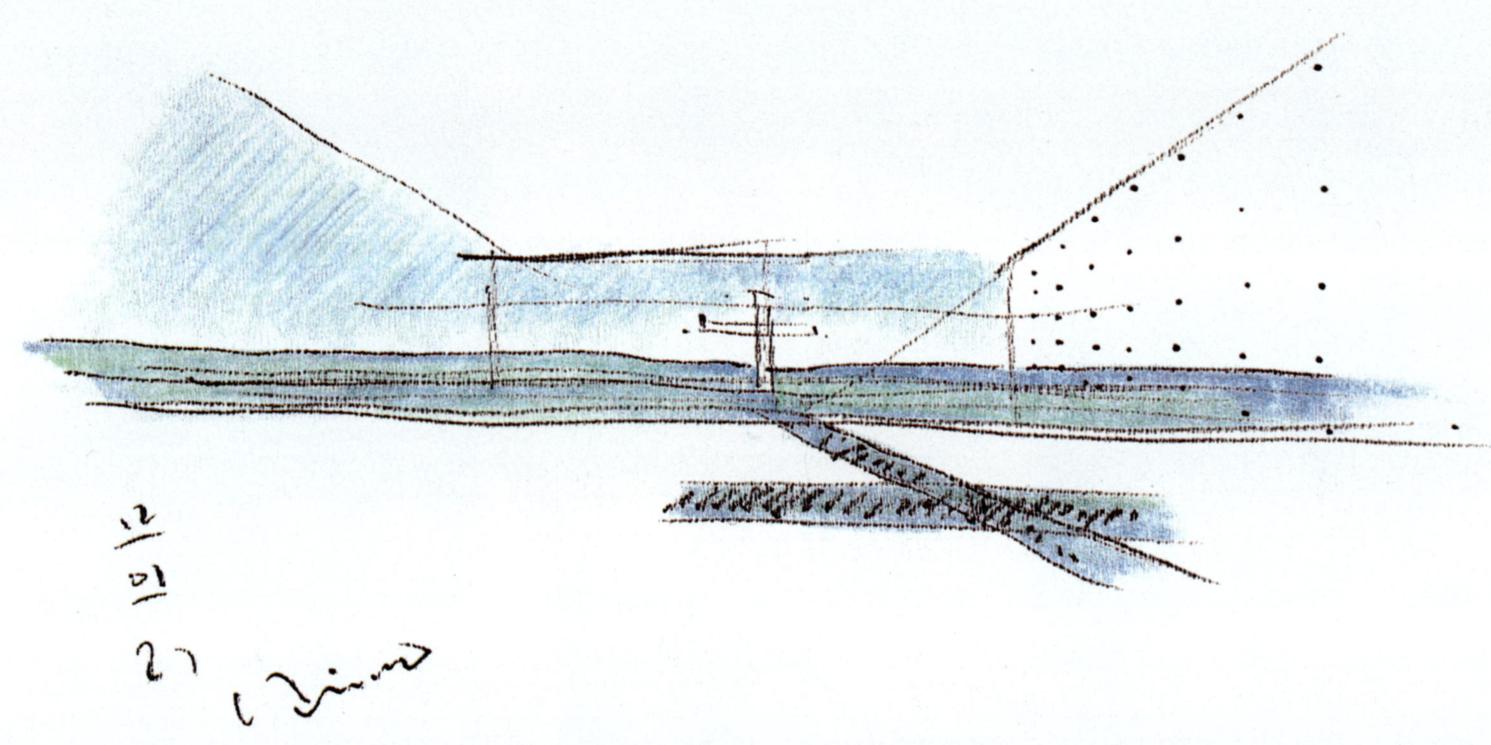

TADAO ANDO: Primary study drawing for Church on the Water, Hokkaido, Japan. *Crayon on rice paper.* [*Courtesy Tadao Ando Architect & Associates* (*Japan*).]

TADAO ANDO: Primary study drawing for Church on the Water, Hokkaido, Japan. *Crayon on rice paper.* [*Courtesy Tadao Ando Architect & Associates* (*Japan*).]

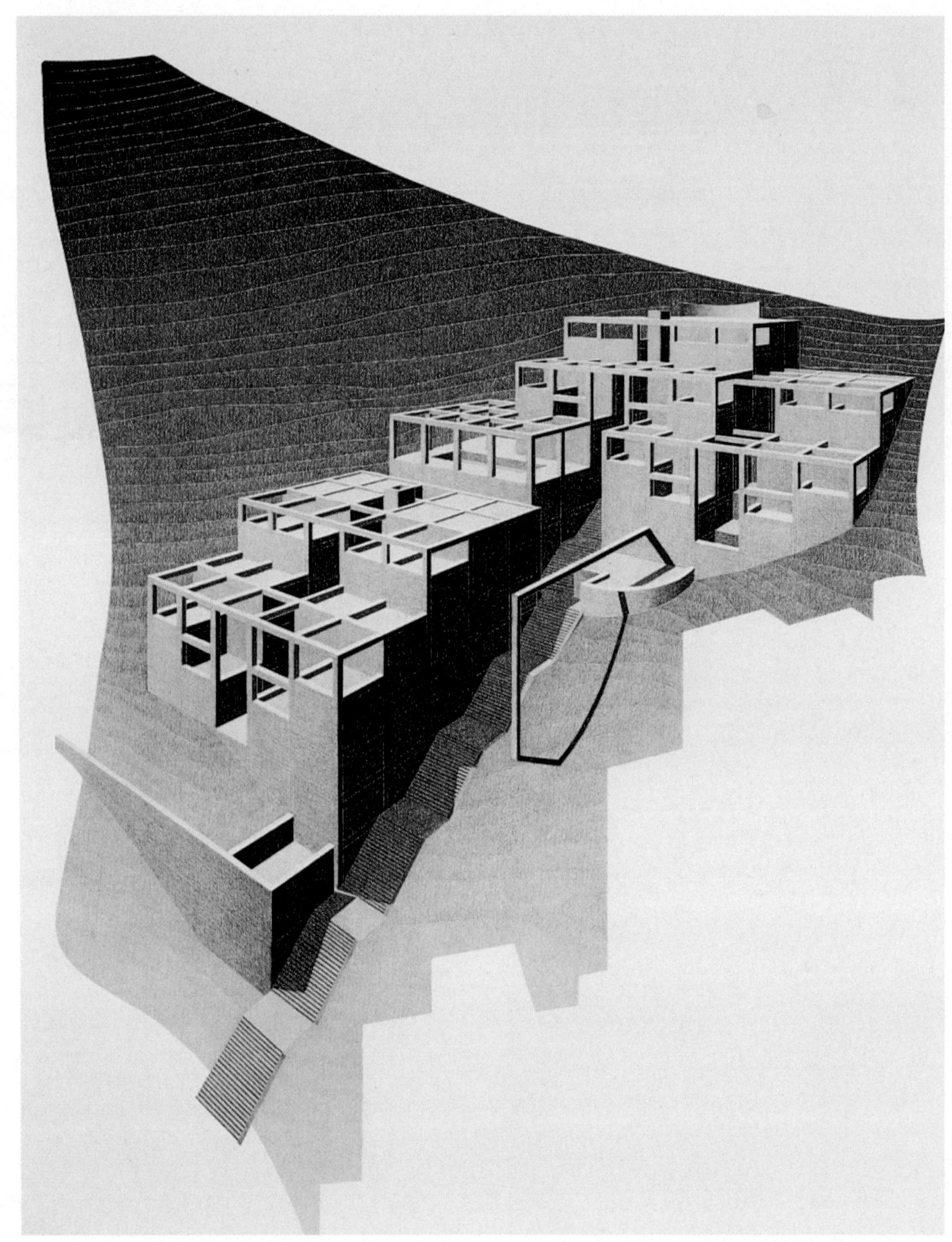

TADAO ANDO: Study drawing for Rokko Housing II, Kobe, Japan. *Pencil on lithograph print.* [*Courtesy Tadao Ando Architect & Associates* (*Japan*).]

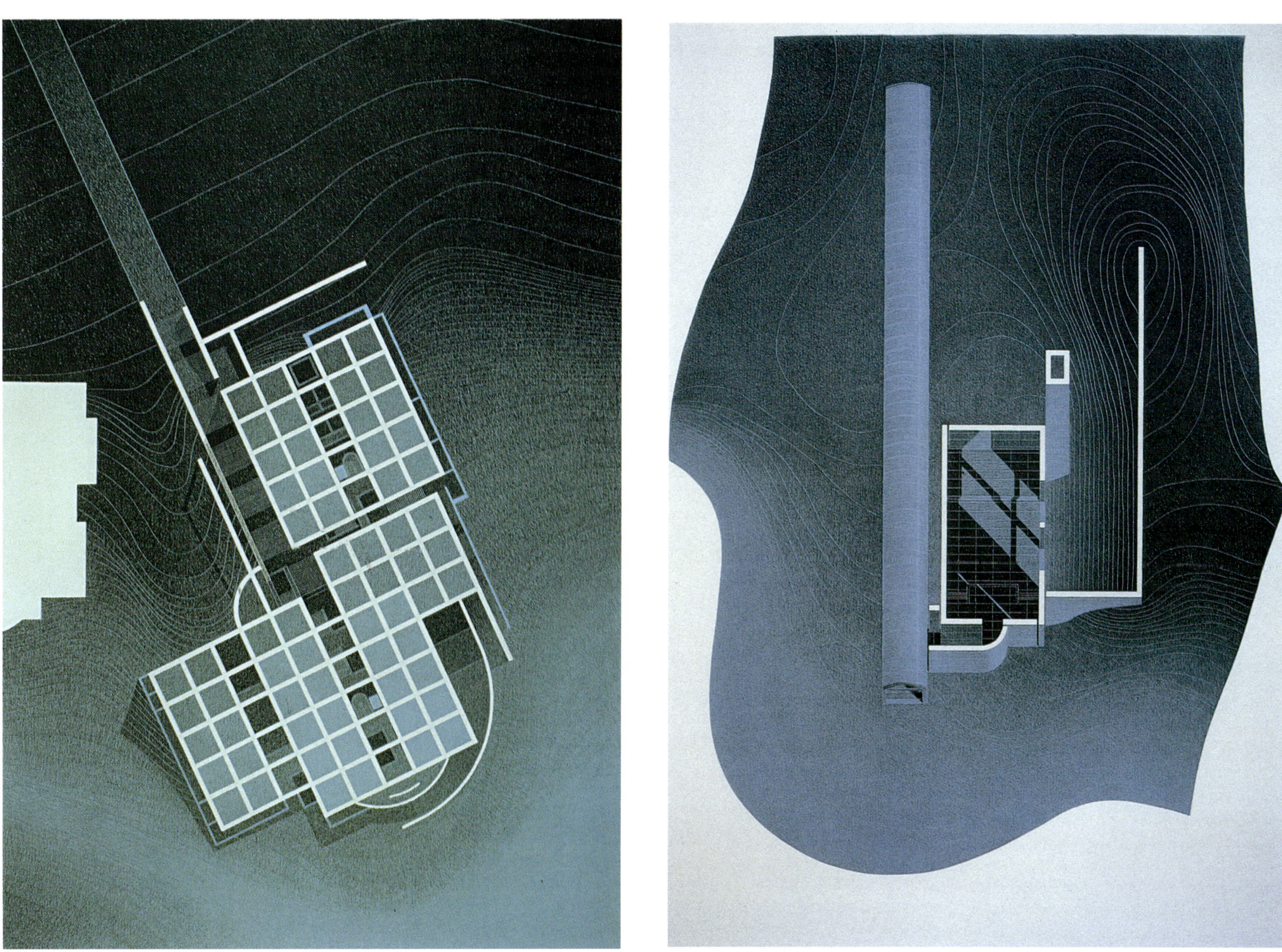

TADAO ANDO: Study drawings for Rokko Housing II, Kobe, Japan. *Pencil on lithograph print.* [*Courtesy Tadao Ando Architect & Associates* (*Japan*).]

TADAO ANDO: Study drawing for Church of the Light, Osaka, Japan. *Pencil on lithograph print.* [*Courtesy Tadao Ando Architect & Associates (Japan).*]

TADAO ANDO: Study drawing for Theater on the Water, Hokkaido, Japan. *Pencil on lithograph print.* [*Courtesy Tadao Ando Architect & Associates (Japan).*]

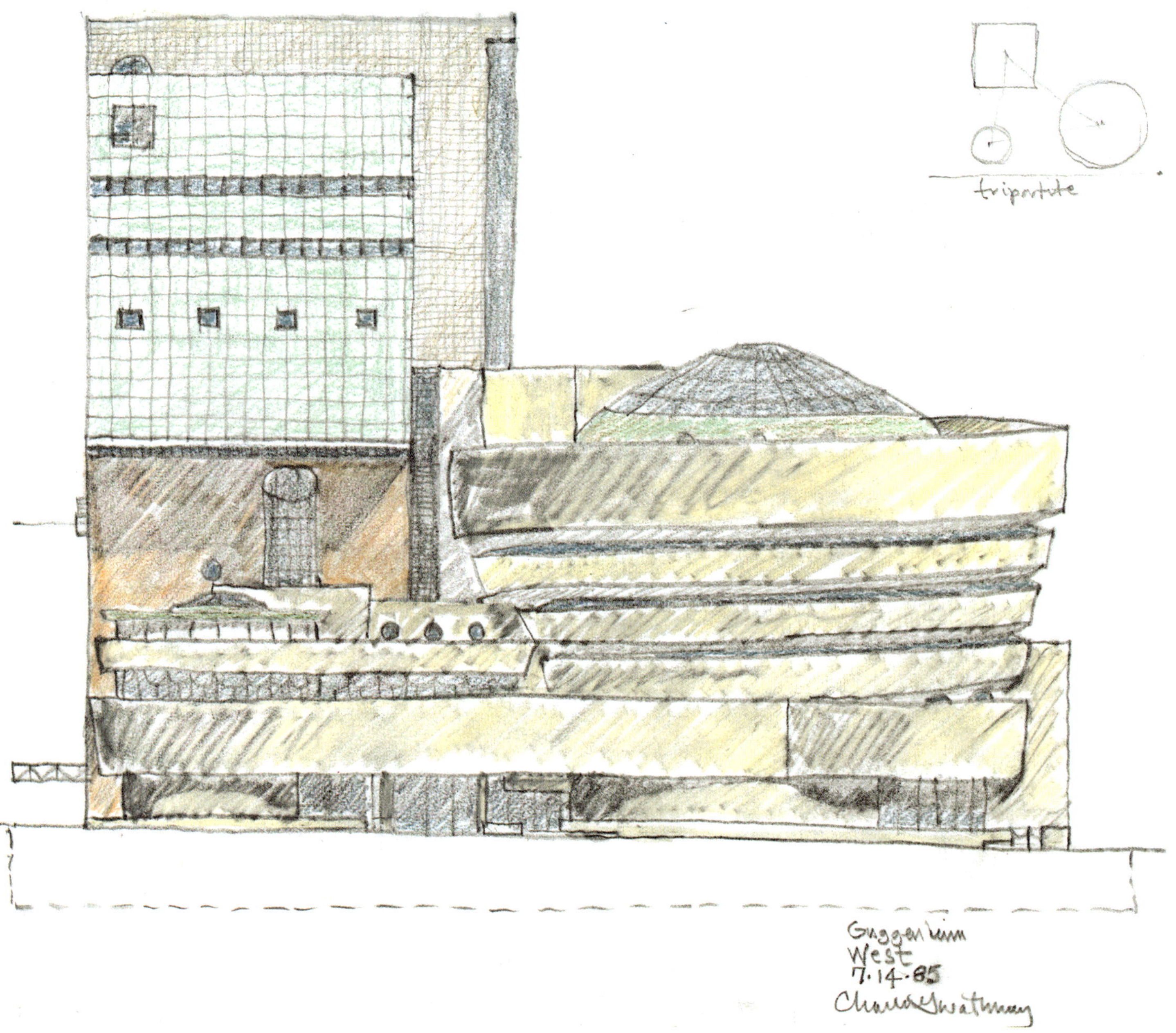

CHARLES GWATHMEY: Study drawing for Guggenheim Museum Addition, New York. *Pencil, color pencil, and ink on tracing paper.* [*Courtesy Gwathmey Siegel & Associates.*]

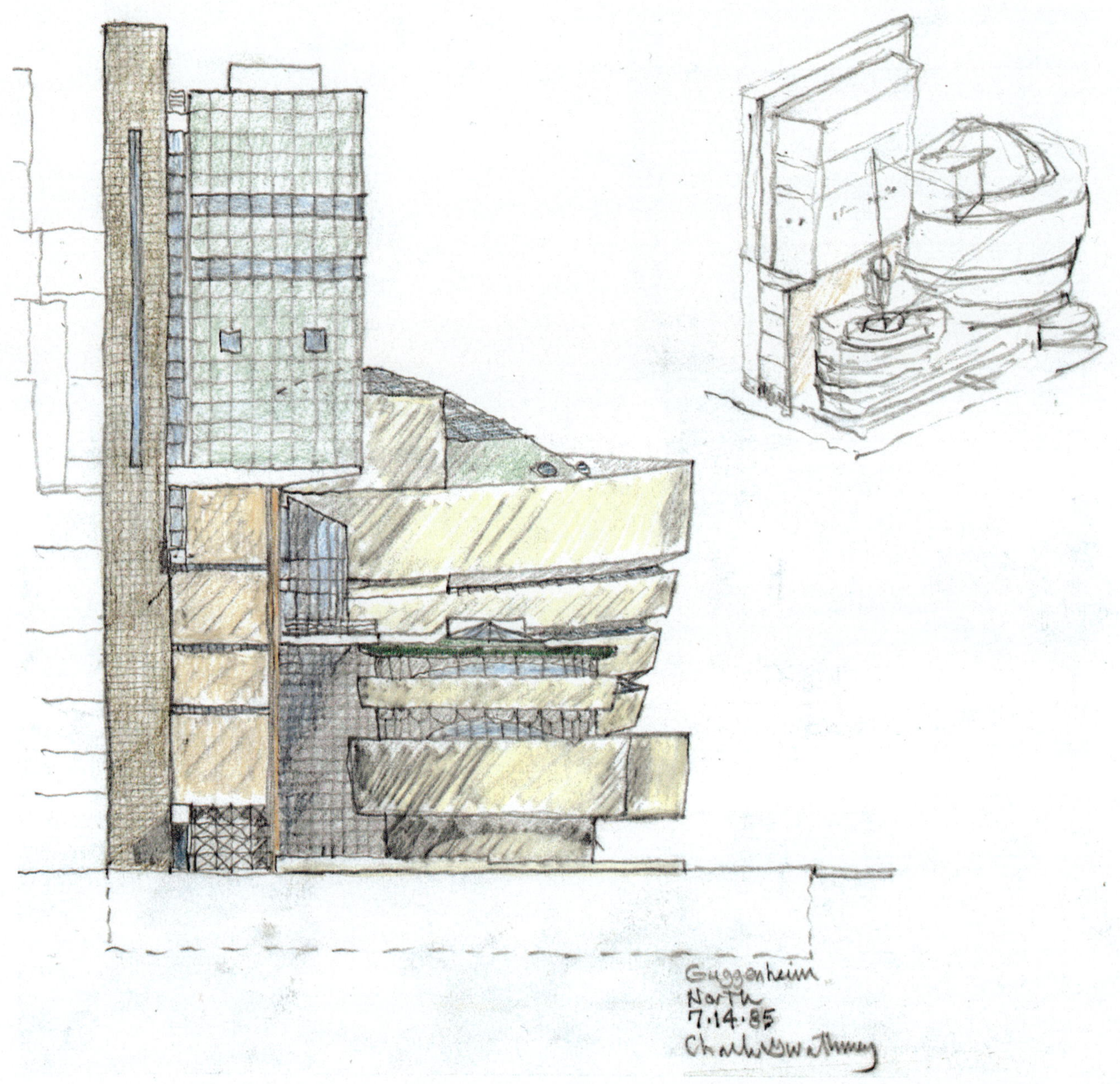

CHARLES GWATHMEY: Study drawing for Guggenheim Museum Addition, New York. *Pencil, color pencil, and ink on tracing paper.* [*Courtesy Gwathmey Siegel & Associates.*]

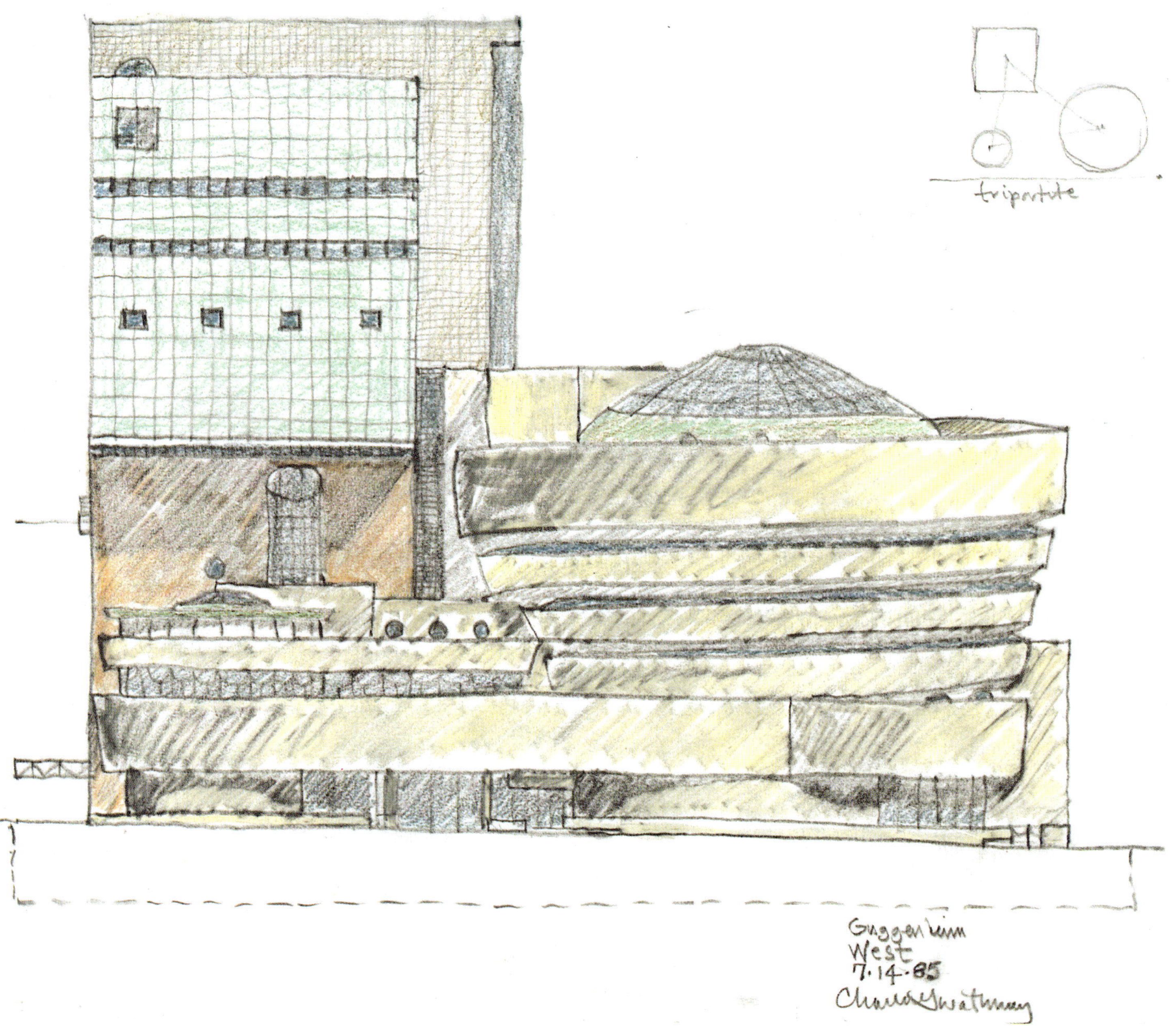

CHARLES GWATHMEY: Study drawing for Guggenheim Museum Addition, New York. *Pencil, color pencil, and ink on tracing paper.* [*Courtesy Gwathmey Siegel & Associates.*]

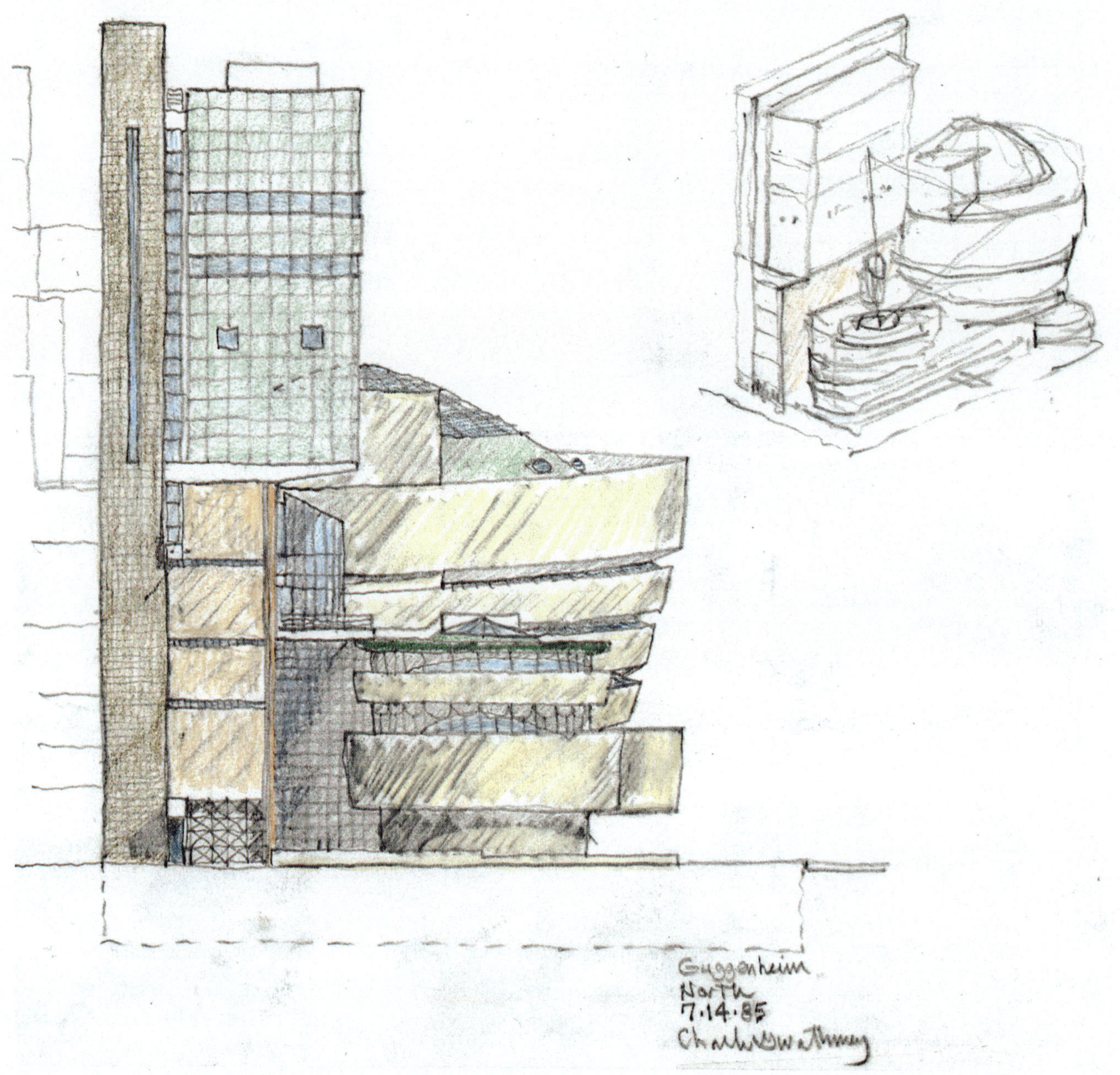

CHARLES GWATHMEY: Study drawing for Guggenheim Museum Addition, New York. *Pencil, color pencil, and ink on tracing paper.* [*Courtesy Gwathmey Siegel & Associates.*]

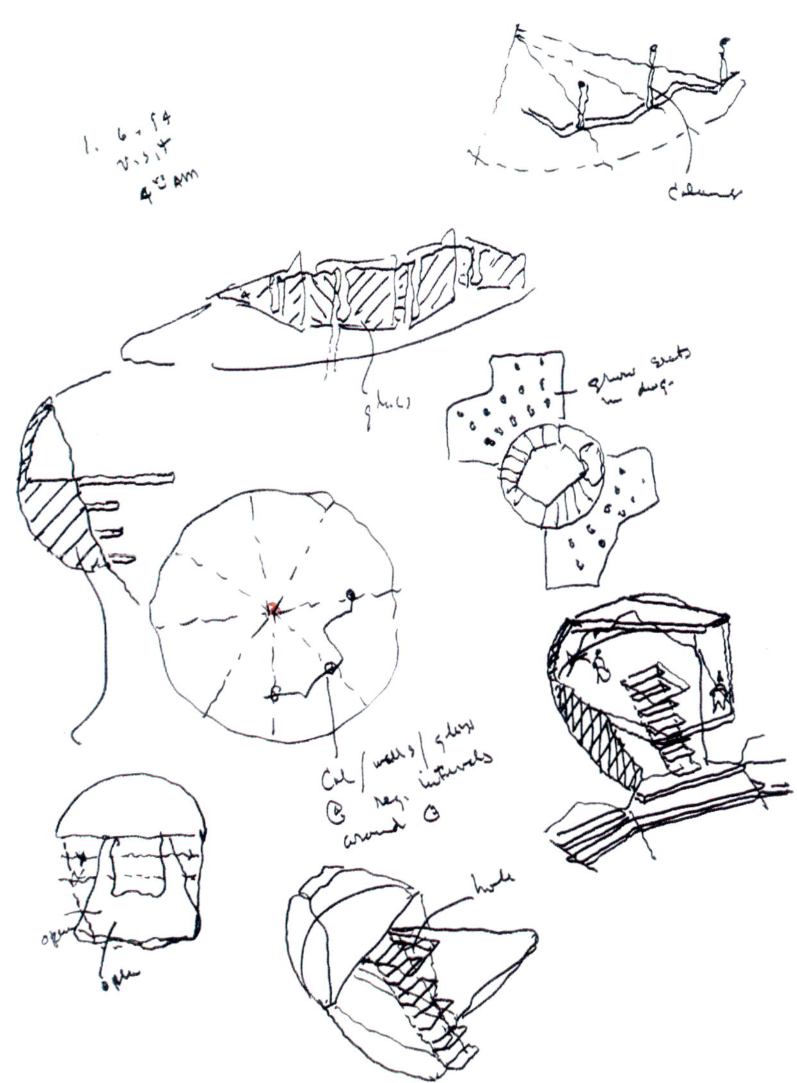

ERIC OWEN MOSS: Study drawing for Vesey Street Turnaround, Battery Park City, New York. *Black and red felt tip pen on bond paper. [Courtesy Eric Owen Moss Architects.]*

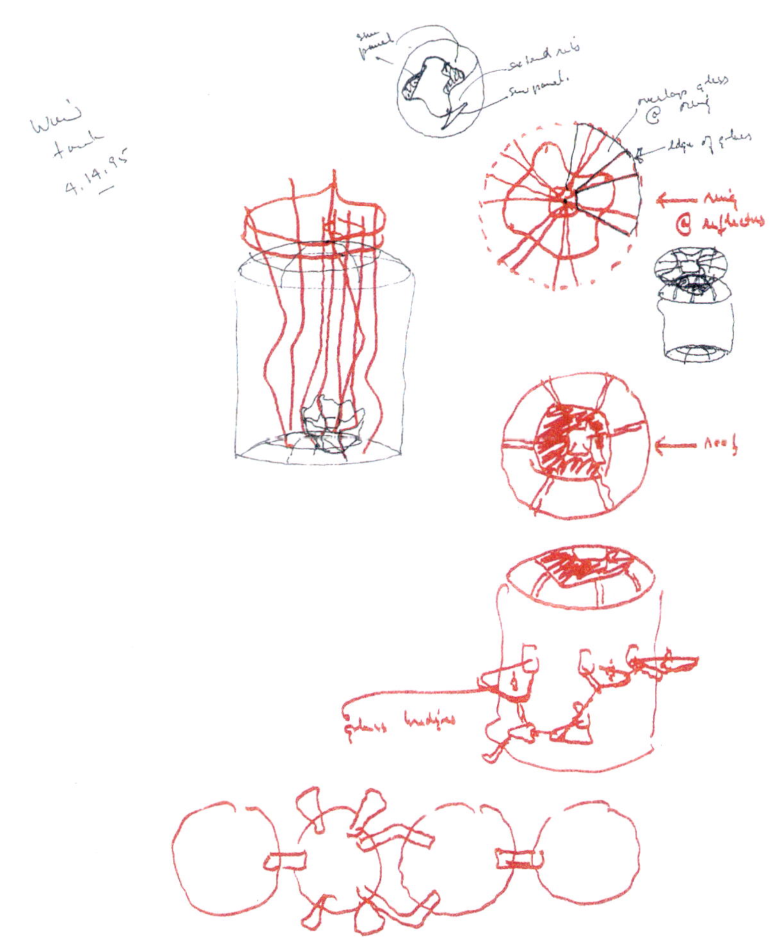

ERIC OWEN MOSS: Study drawing for Gasometer D-1, Vienna, Austria. *Black and red felt tip pen on bond paper. [Courtesy Eric Owen Moss Architects.]*

ROBERT VENTURI: Project for Eclectic House. *Color Pantone paper on KC-5 print.* [*Courtesy Venturi, Scott Brown and Associates, Inc.*]

ROBERT VENTURI: Project for a Rural Wine Center, Dry Creek Valley, California. *Color pencil (white, purple, green) and black marker on yellow tracing paper.* [*Courtesy Venturi, Scott Brown and Associates, Inc.*]

ROBERT VENTURI: Renovations and restorations, Museum of Contemporary Art, San Diego, California. *Color pencil (white, green, blue, red) and black marker on yellow tracing paper.* [*Courtesy Venturi, Scott Brown and Associates, Inc.*]

ROBERT VENTURI: Butler Dining Hall, Princeton University, Princeton, New Jersey. *Color pencil (white, blue, red, yellow) and black marker on yellow tracing paper.* [*Courtesy Venturi, Scott Brown and Associates, Inc.*]

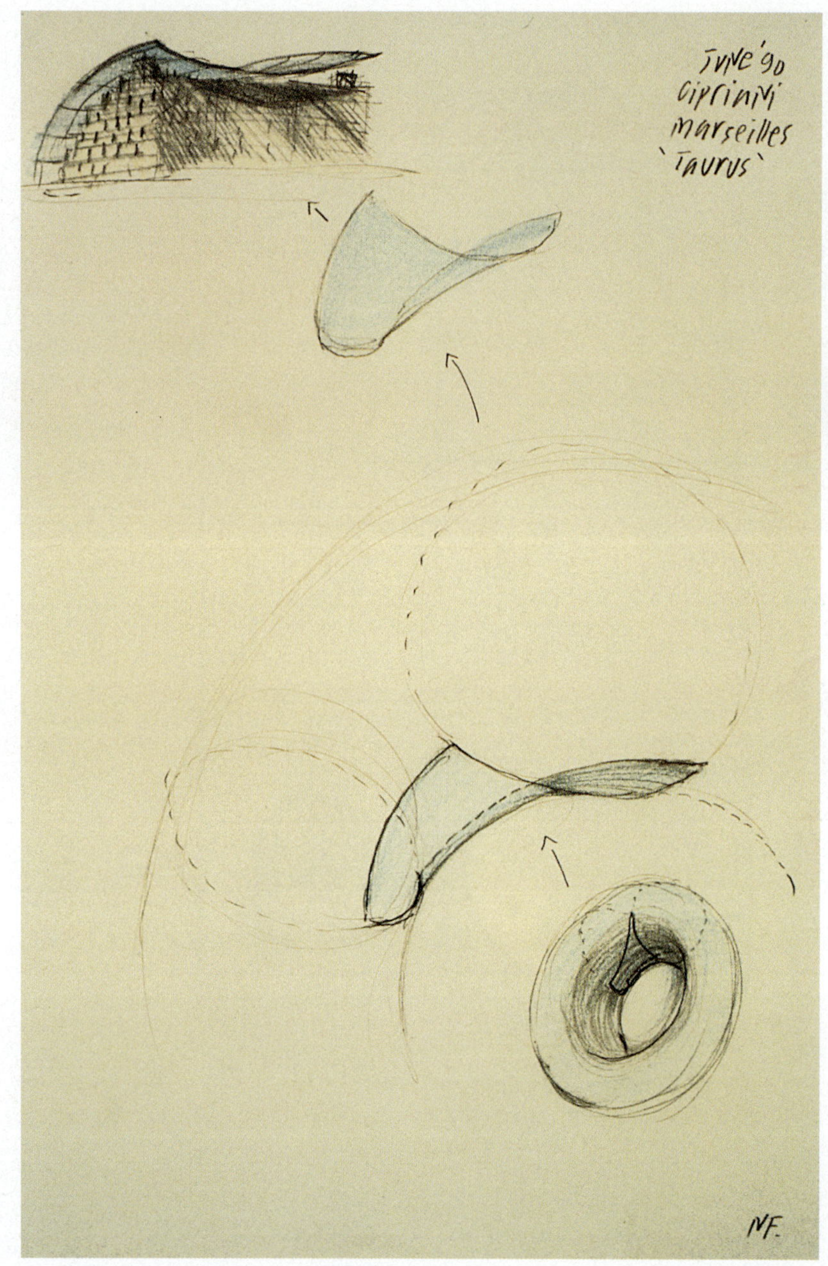

Sir Norman Foster: Concept sketch of Hotel du Departement, Marseilles, France. *Color pencil on tracing paper.* [*Courtesy Sir Norman Foster & Partners* (*England*).]

SIR NORMAN FOSTER: Concept sketch of interior of Hotel du Departement, Marseilles, France. *Color pencil on tracing paper.* [*Courtesy Sir Norman Foster & Partners* (*England*).]

SIR NORMAN FOSTER: Concept sketch of Hotel du Departement, Marseilles, France. *Color pencil on tracing paper.* [*Courtesy Sir Norman Foster & Partners (England).*]

JOHN CHEN: Preliminary sketch for MCI Arena, Washington, D.C. (Ellerbe Becket, Kansas City / Keyes Condon Florance Architects.) *Color pencil, felt tip pen, and red marker on tracing paper.* [*Courtesy John Chen.*]

JOHN CHEN: Preliminary sketch for MCI Arena, Washington, D.C. (Ellerbe Becket, Kansas City/Keyes Condon Florance Architects.) *Color pencil, felt tip pen, and red marker on tracing paper.* [*Courtesy John Chen.*]

JOHN CHEN: Composite study sketch for Barney Circle Bridge (steel arch scheme), Washington, D.C. (Bryant Associates.) *Color pencil, felt tip pen, and marker on tracing paper.* [*Courtesy John Chen.*]

JOHN CHEN: Composite study sketch for Barney Circle Bridge (concrete parabolic scheme), Washington, D.C. (Bryant Associates.) *Color pencil, felt tip pen, and marker on tracing paper.* [*Courtesy John Chen.*]

JOHN CHEN: Study sketch for Philippine Heritage Center, Prince George County, Maryland. *Color pencil, markers, and felt tip pen on tracing paper.* [*Courtesy John Chen.*]

John Chen / Dikang Song: Study drawing for Ronald Reagan Presidential Library (earlier scheme made for Ronald Reagan Presidential Foundation), Stanford University, Stanford, California. *Burnt amber color pencil on yellow tracing paper.* [*Courtesy John Chen.*]

JOHN CHEN: Study drawing for Goree Island Memorial Museum, Dakar, Senegal. (Harry Robinson with Chen & Dunson.) *Markers and color pencil on tracing paper and touch-up on color xerox. [Courtesy Harry Robinson with Chen and Dunson.]*

MAYNARD M. BALL: Georgetown University Master Plan, Washington, D.C. (Keyes Condon Florance Architects.) *Color pencil on Strathmore Bristol board.* [*Courtesy Maynard M. Ball.*]

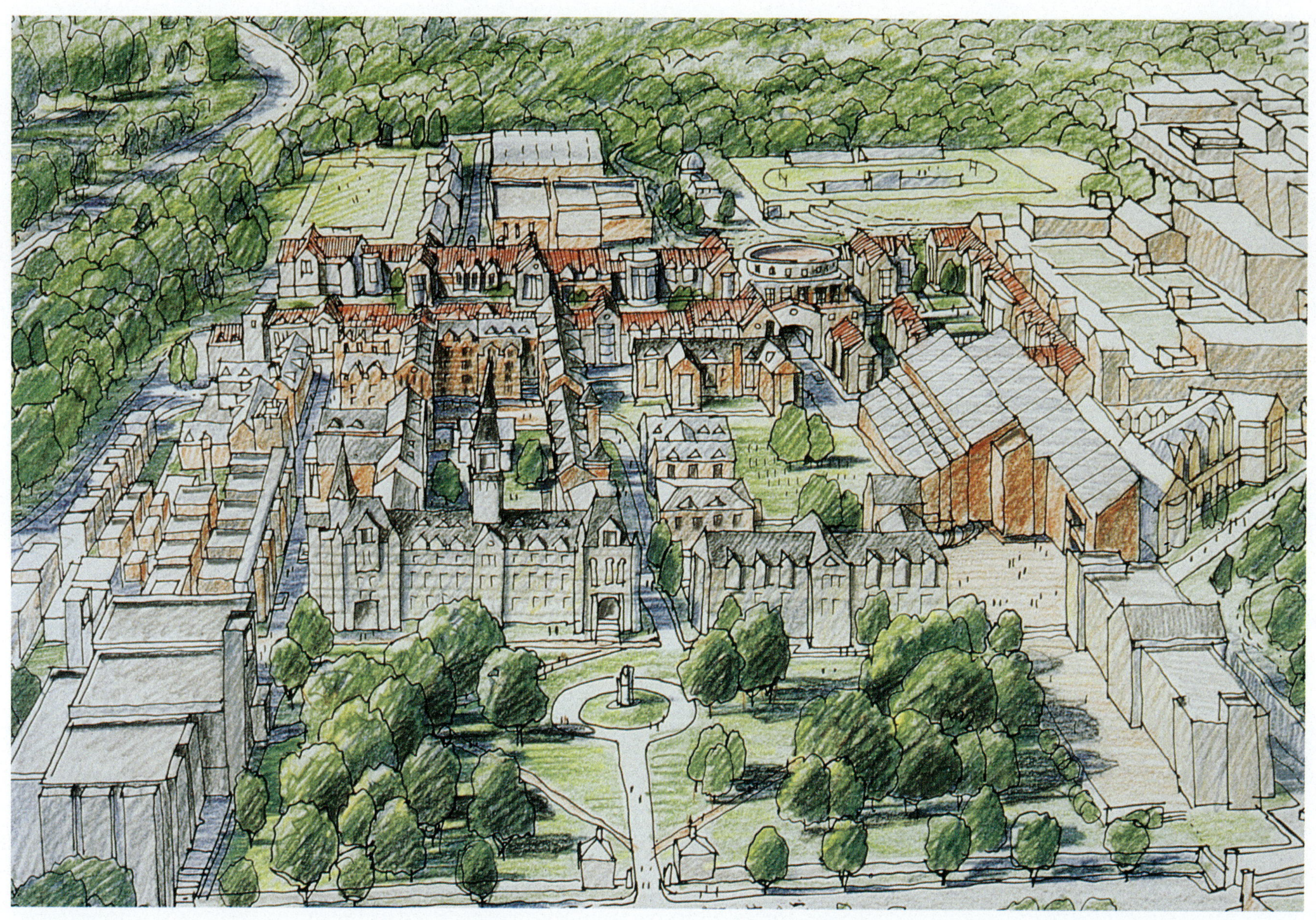

MAYNARD M. BALL: Georgetown University Master Plan, Washington, D.C. (Keyes Condon Florance Architects.) *Color pencil on Strathmore Bristol board. [Courtesy Maynard M. Ball.]*

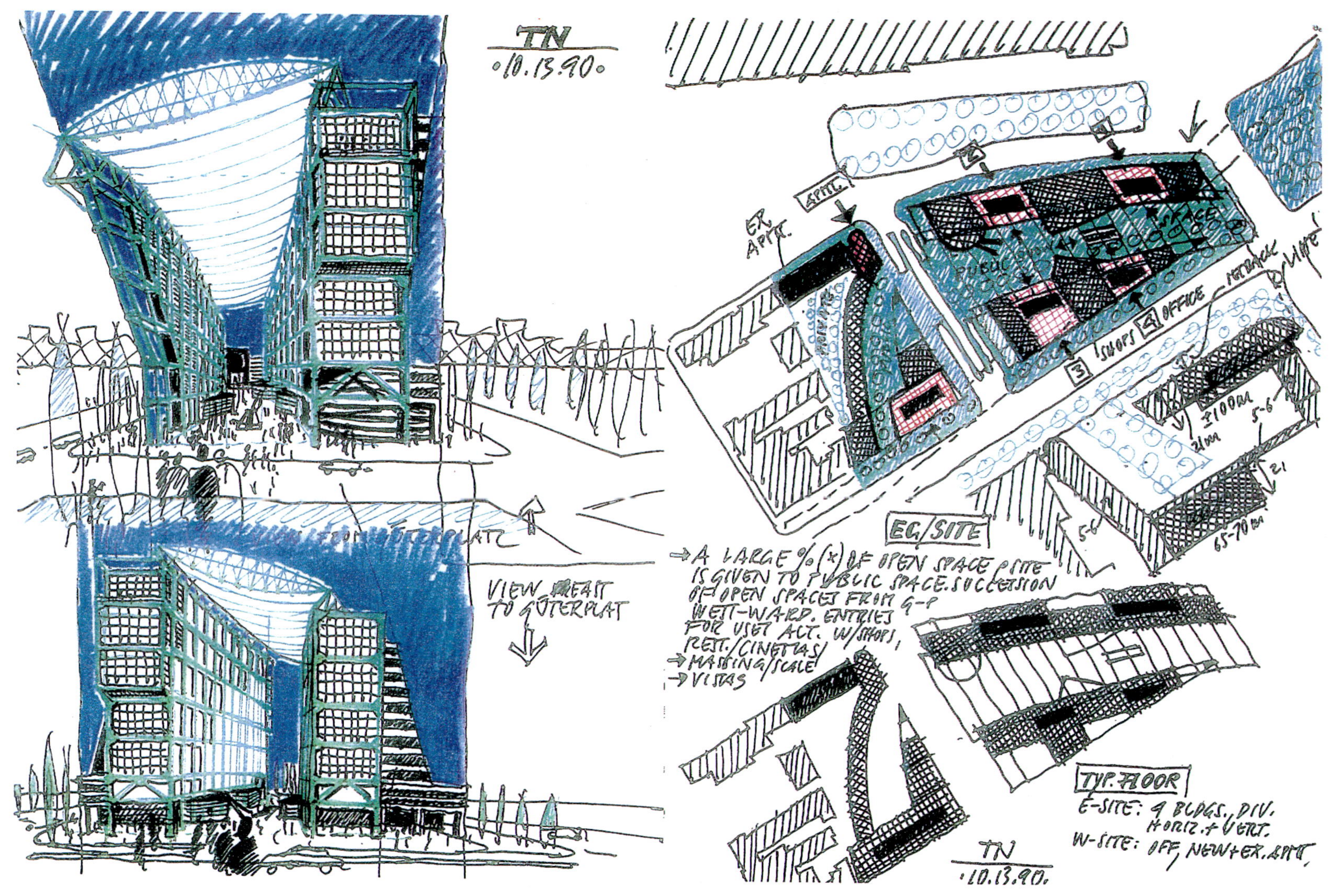

HELMUT JAHN: Study drawing for Europa-Hans, Frankfurt, Germany. *Porsche fountain pen with prismacolor pencils on bond paper.* [*Courtesy Murphy/Jahn Inc. Architects.*]

HELMUT JAHN: Study drawing for Europa-Hans, Frankfurt, Germany. *Porsche fountain pen with prismacolor pencils on bond paper.* [*Courtesy Murphy/Jahn Inc. Architects.*]

HELMUT JAHN: Study drawing for Victoria Berlin, Germany. *Porsche fountain pen, color ink, on bond paper.* [Courtesy Murphy/Jahn Inc. Architects.]

HELMUT JAHN: Study drawing for Project Black, Rotterdam, The Netherlands. *Porsche fountain pen, color ink, on bond paper.* [*Courtesy Murphy/Jahn Inc. Architects.*]

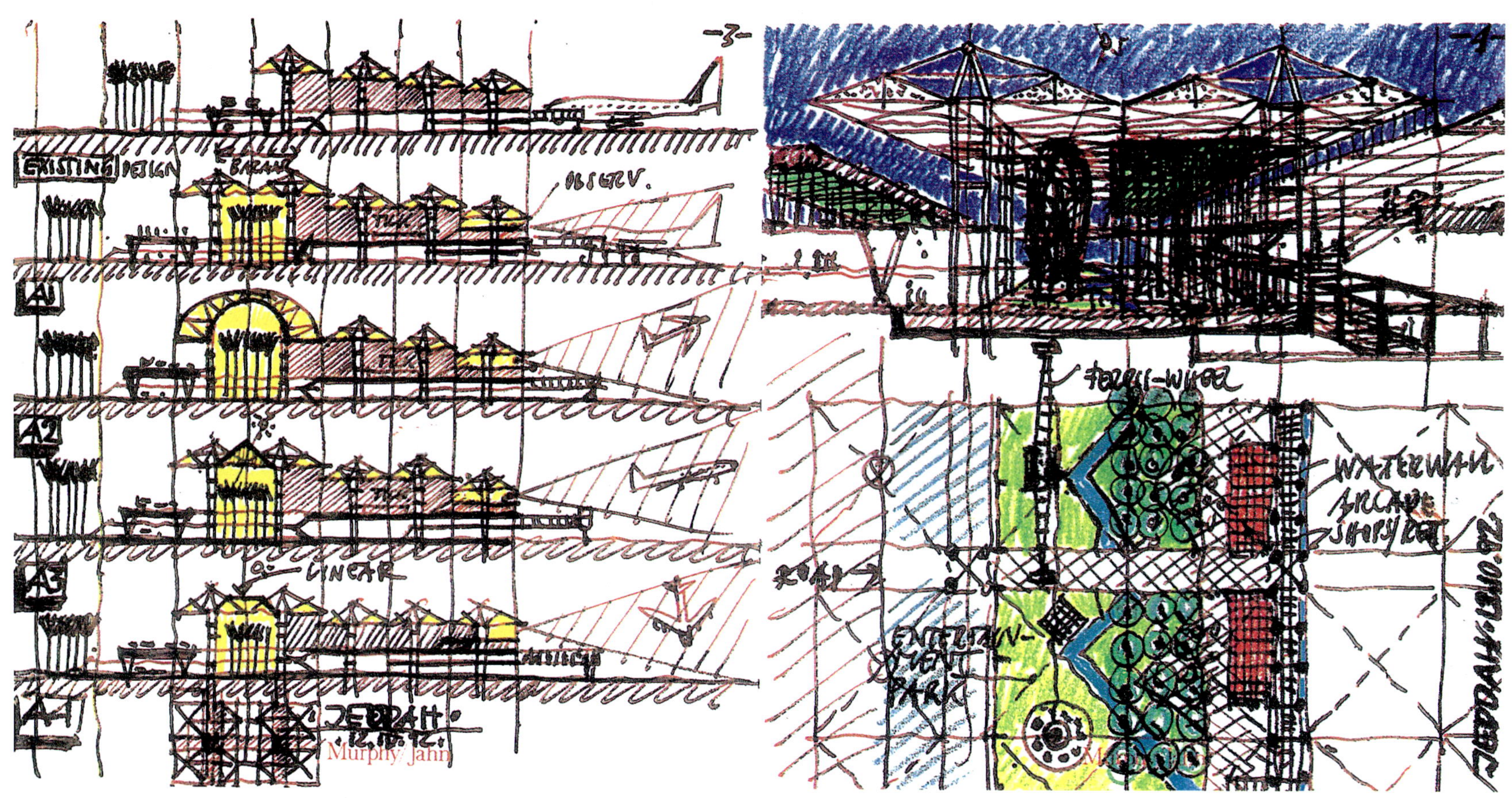

HELMUT JAHN: Study drawing for King Abdulaziz International Airport, Jeddah, Saudi Arabia. *Mont Blanc fountain pen with prismacolor pencils on bond paper.* [*Courtesy Murphy/Jahn Inc. Architects.*]

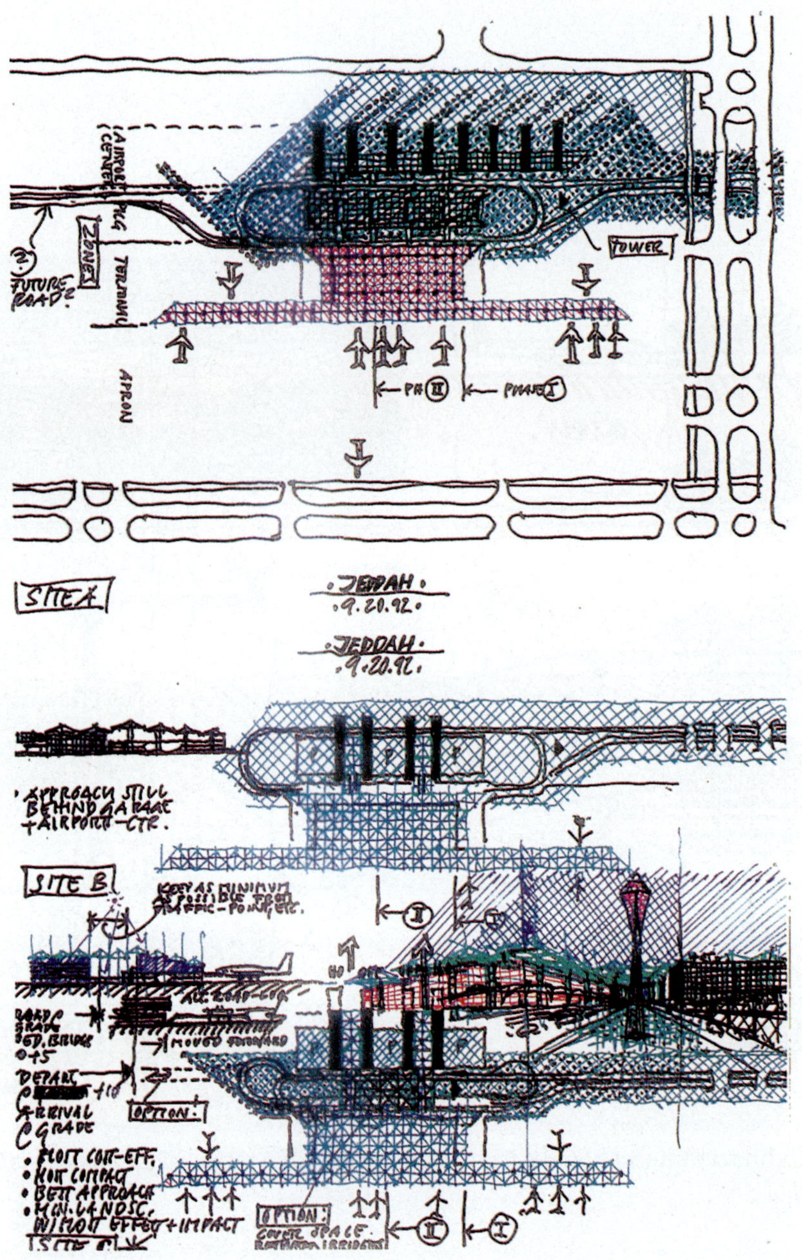

HELMUT JAHN: Study drawing for King Abdulaziz International Airport, Jeddah, Saudi Arabia. *Porsche fountain pen, color ink, on bond paper.* [*Courtesy Murphy/Jahn Inc. Architects.*]

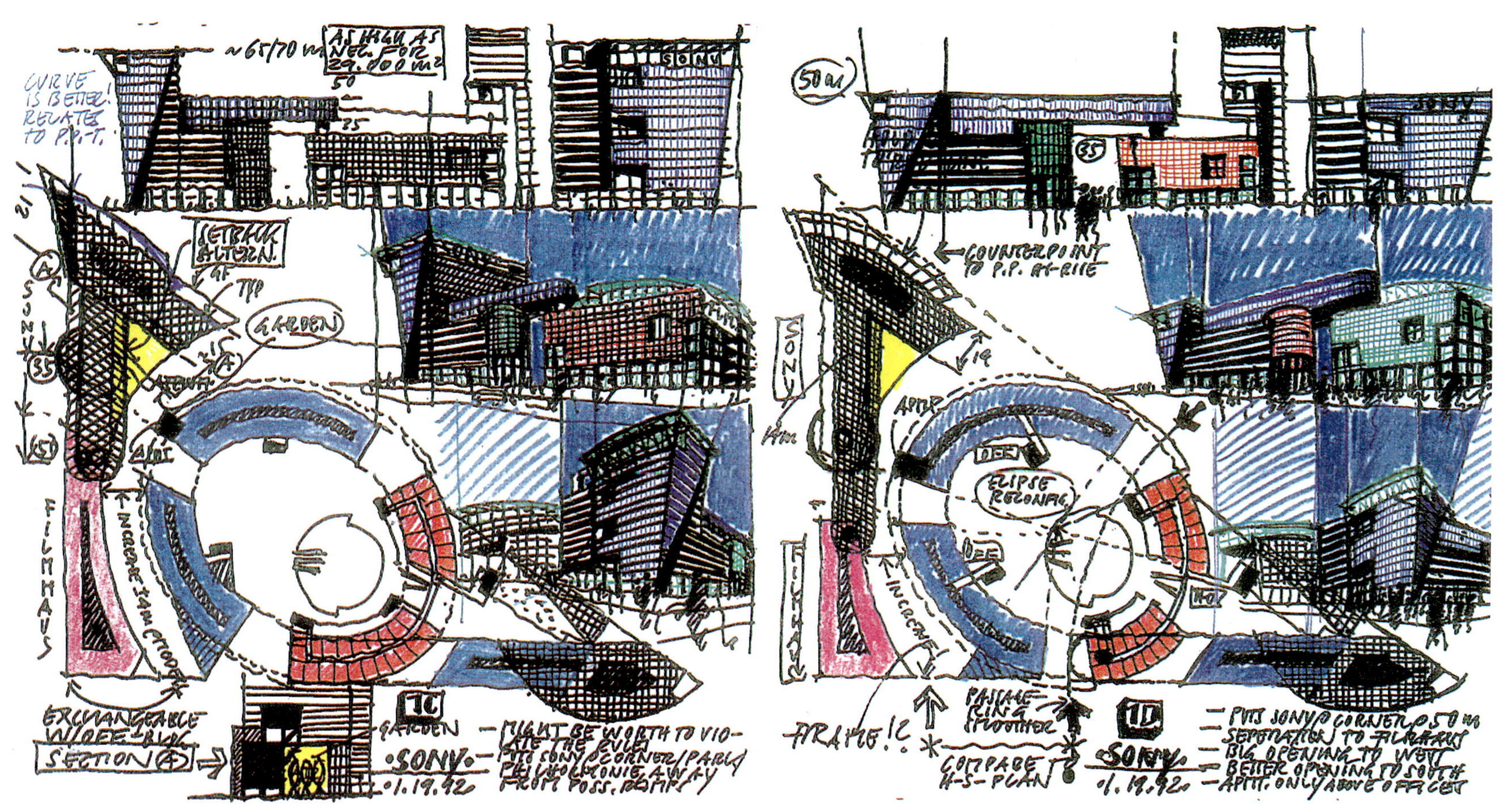

HELMUT JAHN: Study drawing for Sony / Berlin, Germany. *Porsche fountain pen with prismacolor pencils on bond paper.* [*Courtesy Murphy/Jahn Inc. Architects.*]

HELMUT JAHN: Study drawing for Sony/Berlin, Germany. *Porsche fountain pen with prismacolor pencils on bond paper.* [*Courtesy Murphy/Jahn Inc. Architects.*]

HELMUT JAHN: Study drawings for Yokohama Harbor, Japan. *Mont Blanc fountain pen with prismacolor pencils on bond paper.* [*Courtesy Murphy/Jahn Inc. Architects.*]

YI GANG PENG: Composite study drawing for teahouse, Ping Du Garden, Ping Du, Shandong Province, China. *Lead pencil wireframe on tracing paper xerox copy on bond paper color pencil on xerox.* [*Courtesy Yi Gang Peng* (*China*).]

Yi Gang Peng: Composite study drawing for gate, Ping Du Garden, Ping Du, Shandong Province, China. *Lead pencil wireframe on tracing paper xerox copy on bond paper color pencil on xerox.* [Courtesy Yi Gang Peng (China).]

ARTHUR COTTON MOORE: Study drawing for Museum of Art in Glass, Corning, New York. *Watercolor and acrylics on gray board.* [*Courtesy Arthur Cotton Moore/Associates, P.C., Architects, Planners.*]

ARTHUR COTTON MOORE: Study drawing for vacation house, Pleasant Bay, Massachusetts. *Acrylics on watercolor paper.* [*Courtesy Arthur Cotton Moore/Associates, P.C., Architects, Planners.*]

ARTHUR COTTON MOORE: Study drawing for proposed harbor inside a converted Ford assembly plant rehabilitated for housing, Alexandria, Virginia. *Watercolor and acrylics on gray board.* [*Courtesy Arthur Cotton Moore/Associates, P.C., Architects, Planners.*]

ANTOINE PREDOCK: Study drawing for Spencer Theater for the Performing Arts, Alto, New Mexico. *Oil pastel and ink on sketchbook paper.* [*Courtesy Antoine Predock.*]

ANTOINE PREDOCK: Study drawing for Arizona Science Museum, Phoenix, Arizona. *Oil pastel and ink on sketchbook paper.* [*Courtesy Antoine Predock.*]

ANTOINE PREDOCK: Study drawing for Museum of Science and Industry, Tampa, Florida. *Oil pastel and ink on sketchbook paper.* [*Courtesy Antoine Predock.*]

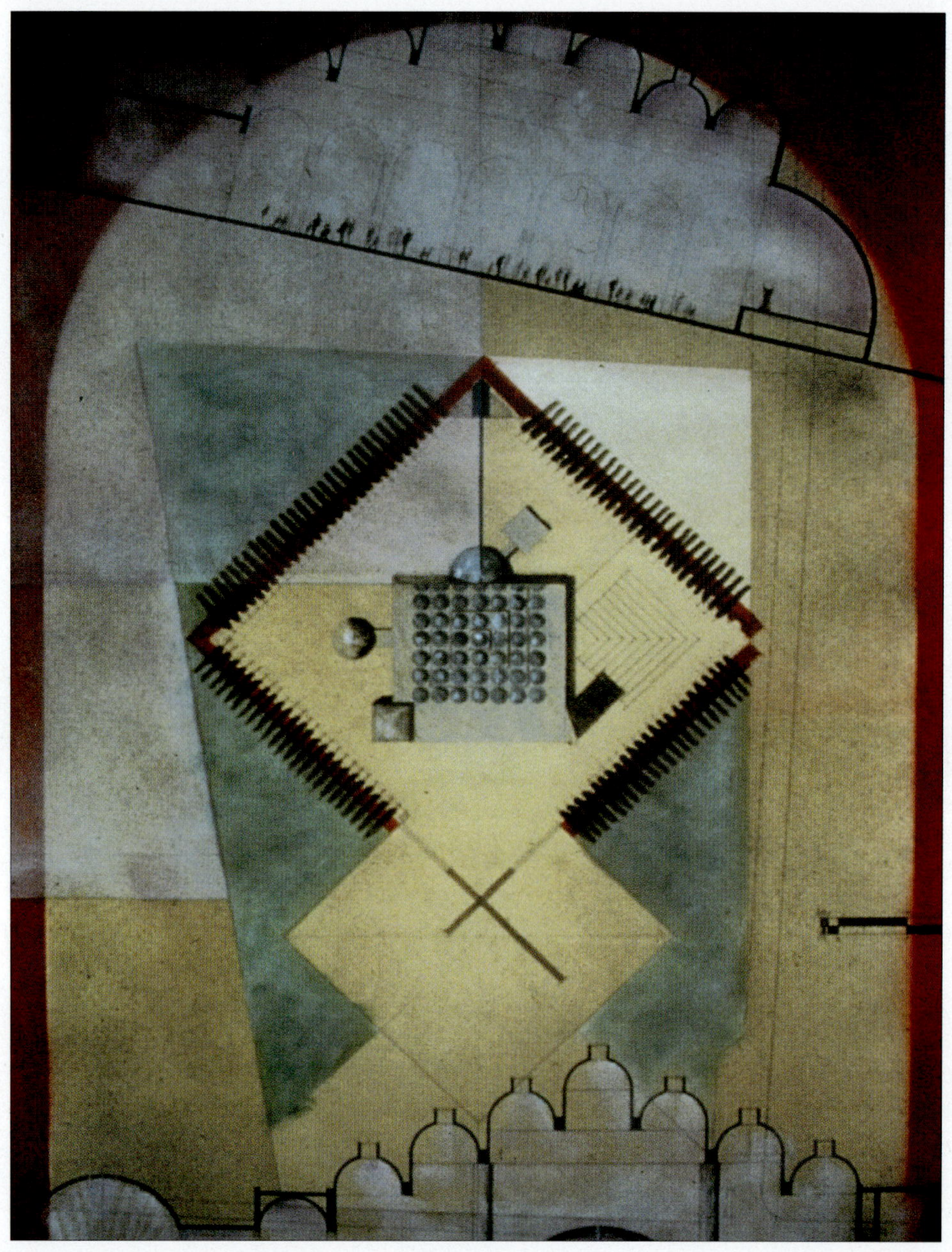

RICARDO LEGORRETA / ARMANDO CHAVEZ: Study drawing for the Catedral de Managua, Nicaragua. *Crayon on drawing paper.* [*Courtesy Legorreta Arquitectos* (*Mexico*).]

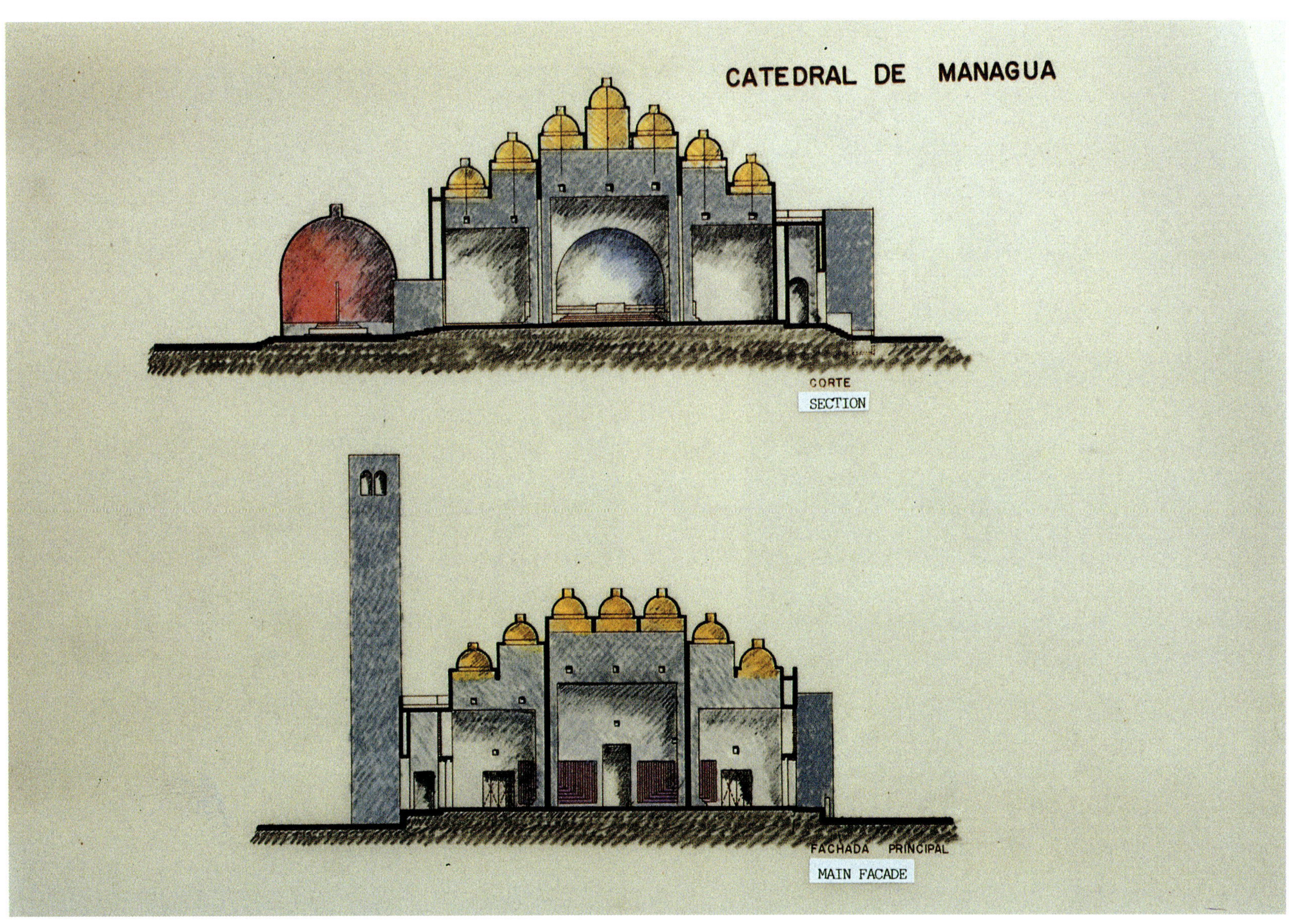

RICARDO LEGORRETA / ARMANDO CHAVEZ: Study drawing for the Catedral de Managua, Nicaragua. *Crayon on drawing paper.* [*Courtesy Legorreta Arquitectos* (*Mexico*).]

WILLEM VAN DEN HOED: Study drawing (untitled). *Markers and watercolor pencils on mylar.* [*Courtesy Willem van den Hoed* (*The Netherlands*).]

WILLEM VAN DEN HOED: Study drawing, III-9. *Watercolor on watercolor paper.* [*Courtesy Willem van den Hoed* (*The Netherlands*).]

WILLEM VAN DEN HOED: Design sketch for apartment complex in Heemskerk, The Netherlands. *Markers and watercolor pencils on mylar.* [*Courtesy Willem van den Hoed* (*The Netherlands*).]

Chapter **2**

Field Drawings in Color

Field drawings may consist of different subjects such as streetscapes, waterfronts, village vistas, mountain views, or snow scenes. But since this is an architectural color drawing book, I'll only include those drawings that involve some kind of architecture, whether it is a window detail, a tree casting dramatic shadows on an adobe wall, a vacation house sitting in the background of a setting sun, or an old bridge over a quiet river.

Just as the name implies, field drawings should be drawn on the site. The majority of the drawings selected for this chapter were actually drawn on-site. However, a few of them might have been roughly constructed on the site and refined with reference photographs later. Unlike the presentation drawings, which are depicting the future, field drawings are depicting the past. Depicting the past normally does not bring an immediate financial benefit to the architect or illustrator, unless he or she is well established.

The benefit of field drawings stretches far beyond the monetary issue; they enrich the aesthetic knowledge of the architect or artist, enable him or her to master composition, proportions, textures, color, light and shade relationship, highlight the center of interest, as well as setting up certain moods. People are creating these drawings for pleasure and amidst this pleasure they are training themselves to be better architects or illustrators. The artist turned architect Maynard Ball said, "Field sketches are many times the only way to record specific effects of light and shadow on building surfaces.... As an architect, I have found that in-situ drawings and paintings are useful for capturing minute details of the architecture and the quality of light and reflection on specific building materials. This is particularly true when doing renovation work to older structures such as university buildings. An added advantage of spending time on site is that one has a better understanding of how buildings are really used by people as well as having something to present to donors and clients that is both beautiful and memorable."

Color field drawings are mainly drawn with the following media: watercolor, oil, pastel, and color pencil. Watercolor is a transparent medium, the other media are not. The architect turned watercolor artist and illustrator Richard Fitzhugh has said, "The world I came to know is dominated by perceptions of complexity, variety, change, unpredictability, 'unknowability' and richness. My first desire is to get my work to reflect these realities while at the same time maintaining unity and focus." Then he said: "The language of watercolor has its own vocabulary and rules growing from the seemingly infinite potential of what can occur when you bring water and paint together on paper. To complete the idea, the trick for me is to always be mindful the task is not to attempt to make the language of watercolor mimic the language of reality, but instead to translate the language of reality into the language of watercolor. However skillful an illusionist an artist may be, there is no escaping the truth that we paint with paint." Another watercolor artist, Joe Mayer, said, "When I am planning and executing a watercolor, I feel both the freedom and the obligation to change, add or delete facts which do not contribute to the composition. I wish to create paintings rather than pictures."

The nontransparent media have the ability to be built up layer over layer, creating contrast, highlights, and center of interest. Pastel is a kind of nontransparent medium. Pastels are pure pigments of ground color held together by a binding ingredient. While watercolor drawings are depicting reality in a more philosophic way, pastel drawings are depicting reality at its best moments. Pastel artist Albert Handell chooses sanded pastel paper to form a ground grain and then builds up a texture with pigments. He always carefully studies the patterns of light and shadow and captures them at their most captivating time. Giving prominence to the center of interest, he uses highlights and added contrast to the overall texture and draw more tightly. The background is left simple and subdued, the foreground bold and rough, letting the eyes focus towards the center of interest. Looking at his drawings is like reading poetry, and each one has its own theme.

The Oles/Thompson House, Newton Lower Falls, Massachusetts. Painted by Paul Stevenson Oles. *Watercolor on watercolor paper.* [*Courtesy Paul Stevenson Oles, FAIA.*]

The Parry House, Cape Neddick, Maine. Painted by Paul Stevenson Oles. *Watercolor on watercolor paper.* [*Courtesy Paul Stevenson Oles, FAIA.*]

John Langeloth and Frances Lehman Loeb House, Harvard University, Cambridge, Massachusetts. Painted by Paul Stevenson Oles. *Watercolor on watercolor paper.* [*Courtesy Paul Stevenson Oles, FAIA.*]

Bosco Parrasio, Rome, Italy. Drawn by Gilbert Gorski. *Watercolor on watercolor paper.* [*Courtesy Gilbert Gorski.*]

View of Rome from the Gianicolo Hill, Rome, Italy. Drawn by Gilbert Gorski. *Pencil and diluted ink on Fabrianno watercolor paper, watercolor added in studio.* [*Courtesy Gilbert Gorski.*]

S. Maria Di Loreto and SS. Nome Di Maria, Rome, Italy. Drawn by Gilbert Gorski. *Pencil and diluted ink on watercolor paper.* [*Courtesy Gilbert Gorski.*]

Accademia di Spagna, Rome, Italy. Drawn by Gilbert Gorski. *Watercolor on watercolor paper.* [*Courtesy Gilbert Gorski.*]

S. Maria Dei Sette Dolori by Borrimimi, Rome, Italy. Drawn by Gilbert Gorski. *Watercolor on watercolor paper.* [*Courtesy Gilbert Gorski.*]

Borthwick Castle, Midlothian, Scotland. Drawn by Thomas W. Schaller, AIA. *Watercolor on watercolor paper.* [*Courtesy Thomas W. Schaller.*]

Duomo, Todi, Italy. Drawn by Antoine Predock. *Oil pastel and ink on sketchbook paper.* [*Courtesy Antoine Predock.*]

Town of San Leo, Italy. Drawn by Antoine Predock. *Oil pastel and ink on sketchbook paper.* [*Courtesy Antoine Predock.*]

Villa Barbaro, Maser, Italy. Drawn by Antoine Predock. *Oil pastel and ink on sketchbook paper.* [*Courtesy Antoine Predock.*]

City of Rome, Italy. Drawn by Antoine Predock. *Oil pastel and ink on sketchbook paper.* [*Courtesy Antoine Predock.*]

City of Urbino, Italy. Drawn by Antoine Predock. *Oil pastel and ink on sketchbook paper.* [*Courtesy Antoine Predock.*]

Yellow Brick Bank Restaurant, Shepherdstown, West Virginia. Drawn by Richard Fitzhugh. *Watercolor on watercolor paper.* [*Courtesy Richard Fitzhugh.*]

Building at 10th Street and Massachusetts Avenue, Washington, D.C. Drawn by Richard Fitzhugh. *Watercolor on watercolor paper.* [*Courtesy Richard Fitzhugh.*]

Barn at San Gregorio, California. Drawn by Richard Fitzhugh. *Watercolor on watercolor paper.* [*Courtesy Richard Fitzhugh.*]

National Archives reflected in storefront of Gallery International, Washington, D.C. Drawn by Richard Fitzhugh. *Watercolor on watercolor paper.* [*Courtesy Richard Fitzhugh.*]

View along Columbia Road near 18th Street, Washington, D.C. Drawn by Richard Fitzhugh. *Watercolor on watercolor paper.* [*Courtesy Richard Fitzhugh.*]

Railyard at Martinsburg, West Virginia. Drawn by Richard Fitzhugh. *Watercolor on watercolor paper.* [*Courtesy Richard Fitzhugh.*]

Building on Potomac River, Shepherdstown, West Virginia. Drawn by Richard Fitzhugh. *Watercolor on watercolor paper.* [*Courtesy Richard Fitzhugh.*]

View of shops along Columbia Road, Washington, D.C. Drawn by Richard Fitzhugh. *Watercolor on watercolor paper.* [*Courtesy Richard Fitzhugh.*]

Alley near 18th Street and Columbia Road, Washington, D.C. Drawn by Richard Fitzhugh. *Watercolor on watercolor paper.* [*Courtesy Richard Fitzhugh.*]

View of house and North Mountain, Shanghai, West Virginia. Drawn by Richard Fitzhugh. *Watercolor on watercolor paper.* [*Courtesy Richard Fitzhugh.*]

Mr. Henry's Restaurant, Washington, D.C. Drawn by Richard Fitzhugh. *Watercolor on watercolor paper.* [*Courtesy Richard Fitzhugh.*]

View along Columbia Road near 18th Street, Washington, D.C. Drawn by Richard Fitzhugh. *Watercolor on watercolor paper.* [*Courtesy Richard Fitzhugh.*]

Building at 18th and Calvert Streets, Washington, D.C. Drawn by Richard Fitzhugh. *Watercolor on watercolor paper.* [*Courtesy Richard Fitzhugh.*]

The Fun Factory, Staunton, Virginia. Drawn by Richard Fitzhugh. *Watercolor on watercolor paper.* [*Courtesy Richard Fitzhugh.*]

Private residence, Jupiter, Florida. Drawn by Maynard M. Ball. *Watercolor on Aquarius II paper by Strathmore.* [*Courtesy Maynard M. Ball.*]

Cottage courtyard, Aix-en-Provence, France. Drawn by Peter Edgeley. *Acrylic paint on illustration board.* [*Courtesy Peter Edgeley* (*Australia*).]

Amongst the Trees on Garcia Street, Santa Fe, New Mexico. Drawn by Albert Handell. *Pastel on sanded pastel paper.* [*Courtesy Albert Handell.*]

The Garden Wall—Bandelier House on Garcia Street, Santa Fe, New Mexico. Drawn by Albert Handell. *Pastel on sanded pastel paper.* [*Courtesy Albert Handell.*]

The Bandelier House—A Pink Adobe on Garcia Street, Santa Fe, New Mexico. Drawn by Albert Handell. *Pastel on sanded pastel paper.* [*Courtesy Albert Handell.*]

The Archway on Garcia Street, Santa Fe, New Mexico. Drawn by Albert Handell. *Pastel on sanded pastel paper.* [*Courtesy Albert Handell.*]

The Leaning Aspens on East Alameda Street, Santa Fe, New Mexico. Drawn by Albert Handell. *Pastel on sanded pastel paper.* [*Courtesy Albert Handell.*]

Early Spring on Garcia Street, Santa Fe, New Mexico. Drawn by Albert Handell. *Pastel on sanded pastel paper.* [*Courtesy Albert Handell.*]

Cornor House on Griffin Street, Santa Fe, New Mexico. Drawn by Albert Handell. *Pastel on sanded pastel paper.* [*Courtesy Albert Handell.*]

The Department of the Interior Adobe Building, the Old Santa Fe Trail, Santa Fe, New Mexico. Drawn by Albert Handell. *Pastel on sanded pastel paper.* [*Courtesy Albert Handell.*]

Quiet Courtyard on East Alameda Street, Santa Fe, New Mexico. Drawn by Albert Handell. *Pastel on sanded pastel paper.* [*Courtesy Albert Handell.*]

Adobe House and Garden on East Alameda Street, Santa Fe, New Mexico. Drawn by Albert Handell. *Pastel on sanded pastel paper.* [*Courtesy Albert Handell.*]

The Pink Adobe on Garcia Street, Santa Fe, New Mexico. Drawn by Albert Handell. *Pastel on sanded pastel paper.* [*Courtesy Albert Handell.*]

Gate, Sun Yat-Sen Memorial Park, Guangzhou, China. Drawn by Ying Tian Liang. *Watercolor on watercolor paper.* [*Courtesy Ying Tian Liang* (*China*).]

The Long Embankment, Guangzhou, China. Drawn by Ying Tian Liang. *Watercolor on watercolor paper.* [*Courtesy Ying Tian Liang* (*China*).]

"Mountain Garden," New Hampshire. Drawn by Joe Mayer. *Watercolor on watercolor paper.* [*Courtesy Joe Mayer.*]

"Techworld," Baltimore, Maryland. Drawn by Joe Mayer. *Watercolor on watercolor paper.* [*Courtesy Joe Mayer.*]

"Morning Light," Berkeley Springs, West Virginia. Drawn by Joe Mayer. *Watercolor on watercolor paper.* [*Courtesy Joe Mayer.*]

"Winter Farm," Shepherdstown, West Virginia. Drawn by Joe Mayer. *Watercolor on watercolor paper.* [*Courtesy Joe Mayer.*]

"Autumn Light," South Bristol, Maine. Drawn by Joe Mayer. *Watercolor on watercolor paper.* [*Courtesy Joe Mayer.*]

"Fast Freddie's," Baltimore, Maryland. Drawn by Joe Mayer. *Watercolor on watercolor paper.* [Courtesy Joe Mayer.]

The Road to the Church, Prague, Czech Republic. Drawn by Sergei E. Tchoban. *Rotring Art-pen, watercolor, and sepia ink on watercolor paper.* [*Courtesy Sergei E. Tchoban* (*Germany*).]

SERGEI E. TCHOBAN: Rebuilding of Frauenkirche. The Past, the Present, the Future…three images of the same masterpiece, the Frauenkirche in Dresden, Germany. Drawn by Sergei E. Tchoban. *Watercolor, pen, and sepia ink on watercolor paper.* [*Courtesy Sergei E. Tchoban* (*Germany*).]

Chapter 3

Presentation Drawings in Color

Unlike study drawings, which are drawn at the very beginning or during the process of the design, most presentation drawings (sometimes called formal renderings) are done at the end of the design. They are used to promote the design, to show responsible commission agents, financial backers, and the general public the physical image of the proposed project, its environmental impact and aesthetic issues. In other words, they help to sell the project.

No matter in what kind of presentation drawing, the architect or the illustrator is always drawing "the future"—drawing something that nonexists, and trying to make the non-existent "come alive." For this purpose, the architect or artist is always trying to depict the future as close to reality as possible, and with their artistic touch-up, the images in these drawings may sometimes look even better than reality.

Most formal renderings use water-based media, such as watercolor, tempera, or gouache. The early techniques of formal renderings shown in magazines such as: *Pencil Point* printed in the thirties and forties can be traced to the teachings of the École des Beaux Arts. These renderings are mostly monochromatic, drawn with the brush applying layer after layer of Chinese ink on watercolor paper, then hand-mounted on board. Although these renderings may be very time-consuming, their aesthetic effects are sometimes considered unsurpassable even by today's standards. These drawings always have high contrast, gradation, significant center of interest and identity. We can see this kind of influence in New York–based architect Thomas Schaller's renderings and imaginary drawings, although his drawings are mostly polychromatic (pages 141 to 143).

Early renderings also emphasize the "purity" of media, and mixed media are seldom used. Tempera renderings containing thick pigments can create high contrast. They are so close to reality that even the construction lines disappear but show as highlights on the edges of the building. Watercolor renderings have cleanliness and transparency and the construction line is always visible, depicting the detail of the building. Gouache is something in between tempera and watercolor. Most of the renderings shown in this chapter are of a single medium, such as the full tempera renderings of John Stuart Pryce and Howard Associates (one of the world's biggest architectural presentation corporations), as well as those of Richard Fitzhugh and some of the author's watercolor drawings. In contrast to the early renderings, almost all these renderings apply airbrush technique, creating evenness and gradation that was once difficult for the brush wash.

In contrast to the majority of formal renderings, which use water-based single medium, some architects are trying to mix media and trying the non-water-based approach. These issues will be discussed in Chapter 5, "Time-Saving Color Drawings." These approaches will definitely be time-efficient and many of them have equal effects. Gilbert Gorski is outstanding in this respect; one can hardly tell his color pencil/airbrush drawings from formal water-based renderings. When I was working on the design of the MCI Arena in Washington, D.C., the rendering (page 123) for the arena was done in a weekend by Mr. Gorski in Chicago. Although his drawings are time-efficient mixed media renderings, they are so refined and dramatic that I still included them in this chapter of formal renderings.

VENTURI, SCOTT BROWN AND ASSOCIATES, INC.: Design competition for U.S. Pavilion—Expo '92, Seville, Spain. Drawn by Steve Izenour and Michael Womack. *Airbrushed latex on KC-5 prints.* [*Courtesy Venturi, Scott Brown and Associates, Inc.*]

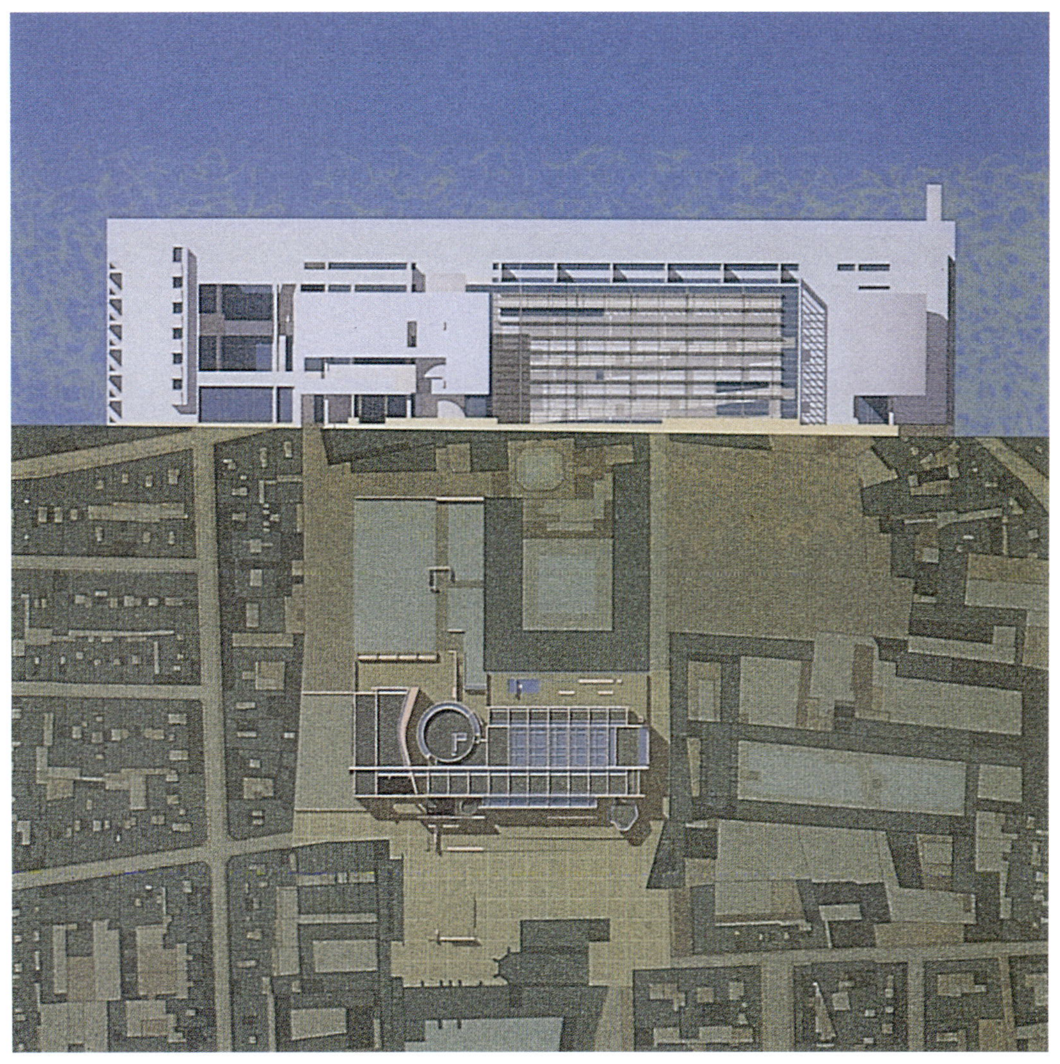

RICHARD MEIER & PARTNERS ARCHITECTS: Canal 1 Headquarters, Paris, France. Drawn by Richard Meier in collaboration with John Nichols Printmakers. *Silkscreen on watercolor paper.* [*Courtesy Richard Meier & Partners Architects.*]

RICHARD MEIER & PARTNERS ARCHITECTS: Museum of Contemporary Art, Barcelona, Spain. Drawn by Richard Meier in collaboration with John Nichols Printmakers. *Silkscreen on watercolor paper.* [*Courtesy Richard Meier & Partners Architects.*]

LEO A. DALY COMPANY IN ASSOCIATION WITH ARTHUR ERICKSON ARCHITECTURAL CORPORATION: Tuntex Brisbane 2000, South of San Francisco, California. Drawn by Philip Sampson. *Gouache over background photo.* [*Courtesy Arthur Erickson Architectural Corporation* (*Canada*).]

ARTHUR ERICKSON ARCHITECTURAL CORPORATION: Abu Nuwas Conservation/Development Project, Baghdad, Iraq. Drawn by Michael McCann. *Watercolor on bond paper.* [*Courtesy Arthur Erickson Architectural Corporation* (*Canada*).]

ARTHUR ERICKSON ARCHITECTURAL CORPORATION IN ASSOCIATION WITH AITKEN WREGLESWORTH ASSOCIATES, ARCHITECTS LTD.: Johor Coastal Development Parcel A, Master Plan and Urban Design, Johor Bahru, Malaysia. Drawn by Robert McIlhargey. *Mixed media on watercolor paper.* [*Courtesy Arthur Erickson Architectural Corporation* (*Canada*).]

ARTHUR ERICKSON ARCHITECTURAL CORPORATION: California Plaza, Los Angeles, California. Drawn by Barry Zauss. *Watercolor on watercolor paper.* [*Courtesy Arthur Erickson Architectural Corporation* (*Canada*).]

ARTHUR ERICKSON ARCHITECTURAL CORPORATION IN ASSOCIATION WITH NICK MILKOVICH ARCHITECTS: Cuhaya—The Sanctuary—House A, proposed residence for an uphill site, Shah Alam, Selangor Darul Ehsan, Malaysia. Drawn by Sonya Lukaitis. *Felt tip marker and pencil on tracing paper.* [*Courtesy Arthur Erickson Architectural Corporation* (*Canada*).]

ARTHUR ERICKSON ARCHITECTS: Cowan Point Resort, Bowen Island, British Columbia, Canada. Drawn by Sonya Lukaitis. *Felt tip marker and ink on tracing paper.* [*Courtesy Arthur Erickson Architectural Corporation* (*Canada*).]

SKIDMORE, OWINGS & MERRILL: Olympia Center, Chicago, Illinois. Drawn by John Stuart Pryce. *Full tempera on illustration board.* [*Courtesy PRYCE Presentation Media.*]

EHRENKRANTZ, ECKSTUT, WHITELAKI—ARCHITECTS OF MASTER PLAN: "The Waterfront at Hoboken" for the Port Authority of New York and New Jersey. Drawn by Howard Associates. *Full tempera on illustration board.* [*Courtesy Dick Howard.*]

THE ARCHITECTS COLLABORATIVES: Proposed multi-use project, Kuala Lumpur, Malaysia. Drawn by Howard Associates. *Full tempera on illustration board.* [*Courtesy Dick Howard.*]

THE STUBBINS ASSOCIATES: Citicorp Center, New York. Drawn by Howard Associates. *Full tempera on illustration board.* [*Courtesy Dick Howard.*]

Jung Brannen Associates: Proposed residential tower on Lake Michigan, Chicago, Illinois. Drawn by Howard Associates. *Full tempera on illustration board.* [*Courtesy Dick Howard.*]

The Architects Collaboratives: Proposed office tower, 5th Avenue and 42nd Street, New York. Drawn by Howard Associates. *Full tempera on illustration board.* [*Courtesy Dick Howard.*]

I. M. PEI & PARTNERS: Gateway Singapore, Singapore. Drawn by Howard Associates. *Full tempera on illustration board.* [*Courtesy Dick Howard.*]

I. M. PEI & PARTNERS: Gateway Singapore, Singapore. Drawn by Howard Associates. *Full tempera on illustration board.* [*Courtesy Dick Howard.*]

HARRY WOLF ARCHITECT: U.S. Embassy, Abu Dhabi, United Arab Emirates. Drawn by Paul Stevenson Oles. *Prismacolor on tone board.* [*Courtesy Paul Stevenson Oles, FAIA.*]

WILLIAM BISSON ET AL.: Children's Museum, Portland, Maine. Drawn by Paul Stevenson Oles. *Prismacolor on vellum with textured underlay.* [*Courtesy Paul Stevenson Oles, FAIA.*]

Sergei E. Tchoban, Hamburg Germany/Sergei V. Zizin, "Sowremennik" Design Association, St. Petersburg, Russia: The Recreation Center, St. Petersburg, Russia. Drawn by Sergei E. Tchoban. *Watercolor, pen, and sepia ink on watercolor paper.* [*Courtesy Sergei E. Tchoban* (*Germany*).]

SERGEI E. TCHOBAN, HAMBURG, GERMANY/SERGEI V. ZIZIN, "SOWREMENNIK" DESIGN ASSOCIATION, ST. PETERSBURG, RUSSIA: The Recreation Center, St. Petersburg, Russia. Drawn by Sergei E. Tchoban. *Watercolor, pen, and sepia ink on watercolor paper.* [*Courtesy Sergei E. Tchoban* (*Germany*).]

SERGEI E. TCHOBAN, HAMBURG, GERMANY/SERGEI V. ZIZIN, "SOWREMENNIK" DESIGN ASSOCIATION, ST. PETERSBURG, RUSSIA: The International Fashion Center in Istra, Moscow, Russia. Drawn by Sergei E. Tchoban. *Watercolor, pen, and sepia ink on watercolor paper.* [*Courtesy Sergei E. Tchoban (Germany).*]

SKIDMORE, OWINGS & MERRILL, CHICAGO: Residential Complex, Ixtapa, Mexico. Drawn by Gilbert Gorski. *Color pencil and airbrush on illustration board.* [*Courtesy Gilbert Gorski.*]

LOHAN ASSOCIATES: Molecular Biology Building at the University of Illinois, Chicago. Drawn by Gilbert Gorski. *Color pencil and airbrush on illustration board.* [*Courtesy Gilbert Gorski.*]

East Pavilion Entrance at the Museum of Science and Industry, Chicago, Illinois. Drawn by Gilbert Gorski. *Color pencil and airbrush on illustration board.* [*Courtesy Gilbert Gorski.*]

Keyes Condon Florance Architects: MCI Arena, Washington, D.C. Drawn by Gilbert Gorski. *Color pencil and airbrush on illustration board.* [*Courtesy Gilbert Gorski.*]

KOHN PEDERSEN FOX ASSOCIATES, P.C., NEW YORK: Internal Revenue Service Competition, Maryland. Drawn by Gilbert Gorski. *Color pencil and airbrush on illustration board.* [*Courtesy Gilbert Gorski.*]

SKIDMORE, OWINGS & MERRILL, CHICAGO: Seoul Airport Competition, Seoul, Korea. Drawn by Gilbert Gorski. *Color pencil and airbrush on illustration board.* [*Courtesy Gilbert Gorski.*]

NIKKEN SEKKEI, JAPAN, WITH DAN MEIS, ELLERBE BECKET, SANTA MONICA: Saitama Stadium Competition, Japan. Drawn by Gilbert Gorski. *Color pencil and airbrush on illustration board.* [*Courtesy Gilbert Gorski.*]

NIKKEN SEKKEI, JAPAN, WITH DAN MEIS, ELLERBE BECKET, SANTA MONICA: Saitama Stadium Competition, Japan. Drawn by Gilbert Gorski. *Color pencil and airbrush on illustration board.* [*Courtesy Gilbert Gorski.*]

TATE & SNYDER ARCHITECTS, HENDERSON, NEVADA: Community College of Southern Nevada. Drawn by Gilbert Gorski. *Color pencil and airbrush on illustration board.* [*Courtesy Gilbert Gorski.*]

LUCIEN LAGRANGE AND ASSOCIATES: 840 North Michigan Avenue, Chicago, Illinois. Drawn by Gilbert Gorski. *Color pencil and airbrush on illustration board.* [*Courtesy Gilbert Gorski.*]

DAN MEIS WITH ELLERBE BECKET, SANTA MONICA: Retail Center, Philadelphia, Pennsylvania. Drawn by Gilbert Gorski. *Color pencil and airbrush on illustration board.* [*Courtesy Gilbert Gorski.*]

DAN MEIS WITH ELLERBE BECKET, SANTA MONICA: Retail Center, Philadelphia, Pennsylvania. Drawn by Gilbert Gorski. *Color pencil and airbrush on illustration board.* [*Courtesy Gilbert Gorski.*]

SKIDMORE, OWINGS & MERRILL, CHICAGO: Shanghai Tower Competition, Shanghai, China. Drawn by Gilbert Gorski. *Color pencil and airbrush on illustration board.* [*Courtesy Gilbert Gorski.*]

SKIDMORE, OWINGS & MERRILL, CHICAGO: Skyrise, Chicago, Illinois. Drawn by Gilbert Gorski. *Color pencil and airbrush on illustration board.* [*Courtesy Gilbert Gorski.*]

SKIDMORE, OWINGS & MERRILL, CHICAGO: Skyrise, Chicago, Illinois. Drawn by Gilbert Gorski. *Color pencil and airbrush on illustration board.* [*Courtesy Gilbert Gorski.*]

SKIDMORE, OWINGS & MERRILL, CHICAGO: LG Kangam Building, Seoul, Korea. Drawn by Gilbert Gorski. *Color pencil and airbrush on illustration board.* [*Courtesy Gilbert Gorski.*]

YING TIAN LIANG: Shenzhen Sports Arena, Shenzhen, China. Drawn by Ying Tian Liang. *Full tempera on illustration board.* [*Courtesy Ying Tian Liang (China).*]

KEMNITZER, REID & HAFFLER ASSOCIATES (NOW EINHORN YAFFEE PRESCOTT): Proposed renovation of the Office of the Secretary of the Navy, Old Executive Office, Washington, D.C. Drawn by John Chen. A color study was done by Richard Fitzhugh. The drawing received a signed endorsement by former President George Bush. *Watercolor on watercolor paper.* [*Courtesy John Chen.*]

Kemnitzer, Reid & Haffler Associates (now Einhorn Yaffee Prescott): Proposed restoration of the Office of the Secretary of War, Old Executive Office, Washington, D.C. Drawn by John Chen, Dikang Song, and Xu Min. *Watercolor on watercolor paper.* [*Courtesy John Chen.*]

HARTMAN COX ARCHITECTS: View towards Elevator Lobby, 1501 M Street, Washington, D.C. Drawn by John Chen/Xu Min. *Watercolor and color pencil on Strathmore Bristol paper.* [*Courtesy John Chen.*]

KRESSCOX ARCHITECTS: Renovation of Colorado Building, Washington, D.C. Drawn by John Chen, Dikang Song, and Xu Min. *Watercolor on Strathmore Bristol paper.* [*Courtesy John Chen.*]

SETTLE ASSOCIATES: Lobby, Channel 7, ABC Broadcasting Company, Intelsat Building, Washington, D.C. Drawn by John Chen/Xu Min. *Tempera and gouache on Strathmore Bristol paper.* [Courtesy John Chen.]

HOH ASSOCIATES: The River Point Project, Northern Virginia. Drawn by John Chen/Xu Min. *Color pencil and airbrush on Strathmore Bristol paper.* [*Courtesy John Chen.*]

THOMAS W. SCHALLER: From "The City." Drawn by Thomas W. Schaller, AIA. *Watercolor on watercolor paper.* [*Courtesy Thomas W. Schaller.*]

THOMAS W. SCHALLER: "Untitled." Drawn by Thomas W. Schaller, AIA. *Watercolor on watercolor paper.* [*Courtesy Thomas W. Schaller.*]

STANG & NEWDOW ARCHITECTS: Stadium Olympics 2000 Proposal, Istanbul, Turkey. Drawn by Thomas W. Schaller, AIA. *Watercolor on watercolor paper.* [*Courtesy Thomas W. Schaller.*]

THOMAS W. SCHALLER: Proposed Hydroponics Research Facility. Drawn by Thomas W. Schaller, AIA. *Watercolor on watercolor paper.* [*Courtesy Thomas W. Schaller.*]

THOMAS W. SCHALLER: Proposed Residential Span. Drawn by Thomas W. Schaller, AIA. *Watercolor on watercolor paper.* [*Courtesy Thomas W. Schaller.*]

PARSONS, BRINKERHOFF & QUADE INCORPORATED: Bridge near Norfolk, Virginia. Drawn by Richard Fitzhugh. *Watercolor and gouache on watercolor board.* [*Courtesy Richard Fitzhugh.*]

HOH Associates: Marlton Manor, Upper Marlboro, Maryland. Drawn by Richard Fitzhugh. *Watercolor on watercolor board.* [*Courtesy Richard Fitzhugh.*]

MIDLAND COMPANIES: Commerce Center, Greenbelt, Maryland. Drawn by Richard Fitzhugh. *Watercolor on watercolor board.* [*Courtesy Richard Fitzhugh.*]

OEHRLEIN AND ASSOCIATES: Howard Hall Renovation, Howard University, Washington, D.C. Drawn by Richard Fitzhugh. *Watercolor on watercolor board. [Courtesy Richard Fitzhugh.]*

M. Saleh Uddin: Rahman Residence, Dhaka, Bangladesh. Drawn by M. Saleh Uddin. *Photocollage using 3-D drawings construction plans and photographs of the completed front facade and interior stair details. Photographs superimposed on drawings copied on color pantone film and negative prints.* [*Courtesy M. Saleh Uddin.*]

Chapter 4

Pen and Ink Drawings with Color

The color pen and ink drawings we are talking about are different from formal renderings. Formal renderings use wireframe and then fill the different planes of the wireframe with color. In color pen and ink drawings colors are applied to the already completed black and white pen and ink drawings. These pen and ink drawings are fully rendered with textures and shadings; they stand alone as perfect drawings, except they have no colors. Since they are preshaded, color applied to them can be less intense.

The advantage of color pen and ink drawings is that one can create different versions of drawings with the same master print, which is the black and white pen and ink drawing. These different versions of drawings will serve different purposes. The original black and white pen and ink drawing is composed of dots and lines. It has no medium tones, the different values in the drawing being due to the density of these dots and lines; therefore it is ideal for reproduction. It could be easily photocopied to make large numbers of prints for circulation or copied to the front cover of a set of construction drawings, which will be used to make diazo prints. Copies of the same master print can also be used to create a series of color drawings of different scenes such as day scene, night scene, spring scene, autumn scene or to show the same building with different colors or textures.

There are different ways of applying colors to pen and ink drawings. Some illustrators apply light watercolor washes over their pen and ink drawings, giving the audience a feeling of gentleness and transparency. Others use markers to achieve the same effect and probably spend less time. Applying pencil colors to pen and ink drawings is also very popular nowadays. They can be directly applied to the vellum that the pen and ink drawing is drawn on or to the print made from the pen and ink drawing. Sometimes a textured board is laid under the vellum before the coloring is applied, thus creating a fussy yet artistic effect. No matter what color medium is applied to these pen and ink drawings, the illustrators normally will not forget to use the airbrush, which helps to create the contrast, the gradation, and the drama.

Rael D. Slutsky and Manuel Avila are two individual Chicago-based architectural illustrators, both known for their pen and ink with color drawings. Both use color pencils and airbrush to color their pen and ink drawings. Slutsky believes that no other drawings than the pen and ink drawing and its color versions can capture in *pointilliste* detail not only the beauty of the building itself, but the foliage, the faces, and the feeling. Both these artists always provide their clients with a black and white illustration which can be used for newspaper reproduction and one or two imbued with color for presentations, brochures, and advertisement.

PEI COBB FREED ARCHITECTS, NEW YORK: First Bank Place, Minneapolis, Minnesota. Drawn by Rael D. Slutsky & Associates. *Technical pen on mylar with color pencil on xerox vellum.* [*Courtesy Rael D. Slutsky.*]

PERKINS & WILL ARCHITECTS: Lobby of Morton International Building, Chicago, Illinois. Drawn by Rael D. Slutsky & Associates. *Technical pen and felt tip pen on mylar with color pencil on xerox vellum.* [Courtesy Rael D. Slutsky.]

MURPHY/JAHN ARCHITECTS: United Airlines Terminal, O'Hare International Airport, Chicago, Illinois. Drawn by Rael D. Slutsky & Associates. *Technical pen on mylar with color pencil and airbrush on photo-mural paper.* [*Courtesy Rael D. Slutsky.*]

MURPHY/JAHN ARCHITECTS: Concourse of United Airlines Terminal, O'Hare International Airport, Chicago, Illinois. Drawn by Rael D. Slutsky & Associates. *Technical pen on mylar with color pencil and markers on photo-mural paper.* [*Courtesy Rael D. Slutsky.*]

HOLABIRD & ROOT: Chicago Historical Society, Chicago, Illinois. Drawn by Rael D. Slutsky & Associates. *Technical pen on mylar with color pencil and airbrush on photo-mural paper.* [*Courtesy Rael D. Slutsky.*]

MURPHY/JAHN ARCHITECTS: 750 Lexington Avenue, New York. Drawn by Rael D. Slutsky & Associates. *Technical pen on mylar with color pencil and airbrush on photo-mural paper.* [*Courtesy Rael D. Slutsky.*]

LOEBL, SCHLOSSMAN & HACKL: Aviation Plaza, Shenzhen, China. Drawn by Manuel Avila. *Technical pen with color pencil and airbrush on vellum.* [*Courtesy Manuel Avila.*]

PERKINS & WILL ARCHITECTS: Loyola University Medical Center, Cancer Research Center, Maywood, Illinois. Drawn by Manuel Avila. *Technical pen with color pencil on photo paper.* [*Courtesy Manuel Avila.*]

LOHAN ASSOCIATES: Shanghai Tower, Shanghai, China. Drawn by Manuel Avila. *Technical pen with color pencil and airbrush on computer paper.* [*Courtesy Manuel Avila.*]

PERKINS & WILL ARCHITECTS: Thomson Consumer Electronics, Indianapolis, Indiana. Drawn by Manuel Avila. *Technical pen with color pencil on photo paper.* [*Courtesy Manuel Avila.*]

HELLMUTH, OBATA, KASSABAUM, NEW YORK: JFK Terminal One Competition, New York. Drawn by Manuel Avila. *Technical pen with color pencil on vellum.* [*Courtesy Manuel Avila.*]

PERKINS & WILL ARCHITECTS: GSA, IRS Competition, suburban Pittsburgh, Pennsylvania. Drawn by Manuel Avila. *Technical pen with color pencil on vellum with textured paper.* [*Courtesy Manuel Avila.*]

PERKINS & WILL ARCHITECTS: Dongbu Central, Suburban Seoul, South Korea. Drawn by Manuel Avila. *Technical pen on vellum.* [*Courtesy Manuel Avila.*]

PERKINS & WILL ARCHITECTS: Sheraton Hotel, Beirut, Lebanon. Drawn by Manuel Avila. *Technical pen with color pencil on vellum.* [*Courtesy Manuel Avila.*]

LOHAN ASSOCIATES: VIP Center, Moscow, Russia. Drawn by Manuel Avila. *Technical pen with color pencil on bubblejet paper.* [*Courtesy Manuel Avila.*]

PERKINS & WILL ARCHITECTS: GSA, IRS Competition, suburban Pittsburgh, Pennsylvania. Drawn by Manuel Avila. *Technical pen with color pencil on vellum with textured paper.* [*Courtesy Manuel Avila.*]

O'DONNELL, WICKLUND, PIGOZZI & PETERSON: Lobby, Chicago Police Department, Chicago, Illinois. Drawn by Manuel Avila. *Technical pen with color pencil on vellum.* [*Courtesy Manuel Avila.*]

SKIDMORE, OWINGS & MERRILL: Design proposal for Croker Tower, Fort Lauderdale, Florida. Drawn by Howard Associates. *Technical pen on bond paper with watercolor.* [*Courtesy Dick Howard.*]

SKIDMORE, OWINGS & MERRILL: Mixed-Use Development Center, New Haven, Connecticut. Drawn by Howard Associates. *Technical pen on bond paper with watercolor.* [*Courtesy Dick Howard.*]

RTKL Associates, Inc.: U.S. Embassy, Kuwait. Drawn by Howard Associates. *Technical pen on bond paper with watercolor.* [Courtesy Dick Howard.]

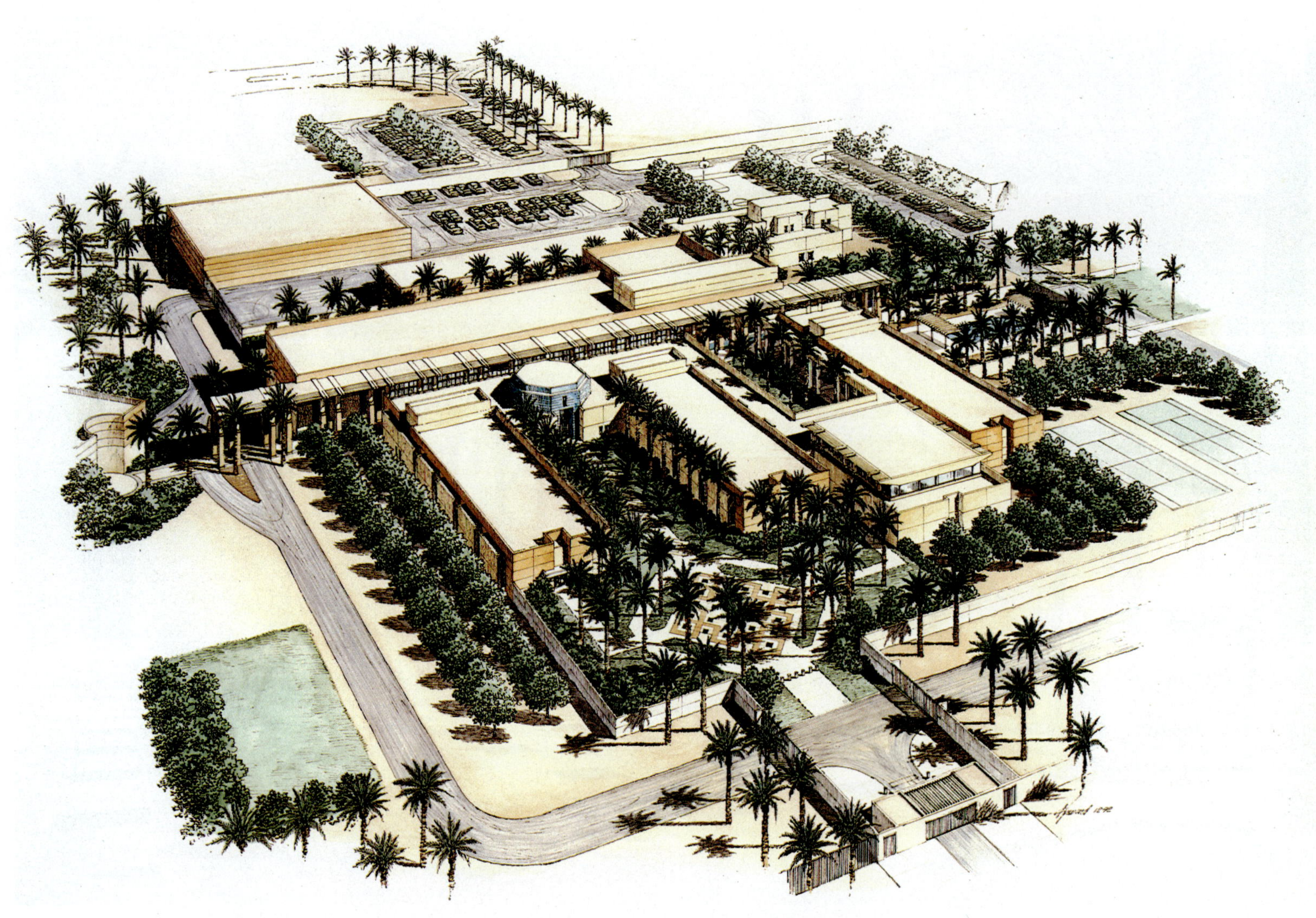

RTKL ASSOCIATES, INC.: U.S. Embassy, Kuwait. Drawn by Howard Associates. *Technical pen on bond paper with watercolor.* [Courtesy Dick Howard.]

LOUIS P. BATSON III, ARCHITECTS INC.: Saint Francis Women's Hospital, Greenville, South Carolina. Drawn by Howard Associates. *Technical pen on bond paper with watercolor.* [*Courtesy Dick Howard.*]

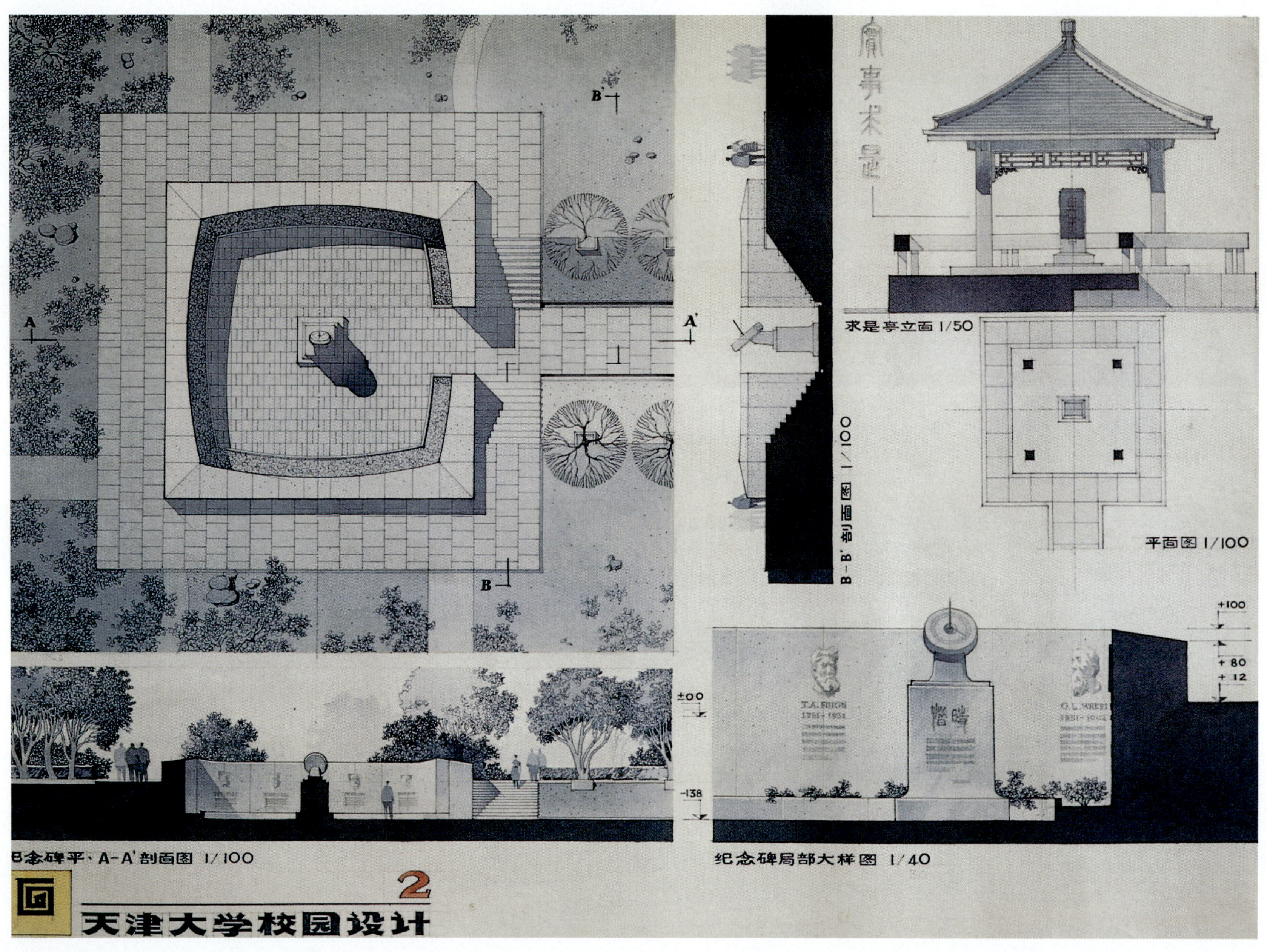

YI GANG PENG: Campus Element Design, Tianjin University, Tianjin, China. Drawn by Yi Gang Peng. *Blue ink wash and pen on watercolor paper.* [*Courtesy Yi Gang Peng* (*China*).]

Chapter 5

Time-Saving Color Drawings

Ever since renderings have been used in architectural design, people have been struggling to make this time-consuming and labor-intensive process easier and faster. This chapter contains drawings that are of equal quality or close to the quality of formal renderings, but take less time to complete. It also contains drawings that do not necessarily require the kind of refinement seen in formal renderings.

The reason that formal renderings consume more time is that they are done in water-based "pure" media. These water-based media are watercolor, tempera (poster color), or gouache. The factors that affect the speed are the time spent waiting for the colors to dry and the time spent mixing the different pigments.

The revolution started by partially or totally abandoning the water-based media. People were able to do this because there are more graphic products available nowadays than ever before. Airbrush and markers were the two prominent graphic inventions of this century before computer application. The increasing variety of color pencils and pastels also enables architects to create non-water-based drawings.

During recent years I've developed a type of time-saving drawing, which is called watercolor look-alike drawings. These are non-water-based drawings, using markers as a prime layer of colors and touched up with color pencils, and if this is not enough I will apply some airbrush to it. The construction of the wireframes is basically executed by computer. Some of these drawings are drawn directly on inexpensive tracing paper, which takes both markers and color pencil well. Due to the transparency of the tracing paper, these colors can be applied to either side of the paper, whichever way that shows the best result. Airbrush is used mainly for the bigger areas such as the sky, streets, and parking lots. I'm also using alcohol to substitute for water in the airbrush; alcohol dries faster and won't buckle the paper, even if it is tracing paper. The electric eraser can be used like a brush creating highlights and is especially good for drawing clouds.

Gene Streett, who draws numerous perspectives for rapid transit systems around the country and abroad, has developed his own type of time-saving drawings. Most of his drawings are drawn on vellum with technical pen or black felt pen with some shading and printed on diazo paper; the artist applies color markers to the diazo later. Although these perspectives are mainly drawn on bigger size paper (such as 24-inch X 36-inch), but due to his proficiency and the non-water-based media, he can draw a rather complicated full color perspective in just one day.

One of the approaches of the Australian architectural illustrator Peter Edgeley is to use photographic cut-outs with airbrush and paint on black color board. It is basically a montage and painting process. The process starts with selecting photographs which are similar to the context, lighting, and mood of the proposal being illustrated. Taking into account the view required, the photographs are cut and pasted into position. The black color board will provide seamless high-contrast background, letting the montage and airbrush stand out. Some other drawings by Peter Edgeley are drawn on heavyweight tracing paper using a combination of color pencil and overlay paint highlights.

Today's architects and illustrators are blessed with an abundance of new graphic materials and equipment; it is up to them to explore new ways of making time-saving color drawings.

OFFICE OF FOREIGN BUILDINGS OPERATIONS, U.S. DEPARTMENT OF STATE / CABELLERO ARCHITECTS: U.S. Interest Section, Havana, Cuba. Drawn by John Chen. *Markers and color pencil on Strathmore Bristol paper.* [Courtesy John Chen.]

Office of Foreign Buildings Operations, U.S. Department of State/Cabellero Architects: View of courtyard, U.S. Interest Section, Havana, Cuba. Drawn by John Chen. *Markers and color pencil on Strathmore Bristol paper.* [Courtesy *John Chen.*]

Office of Foreign Buildings Operations, U.S. Department of State/Cabellero Architects: Consular Section, U.S. Interest Section, Havana, Cuba. Drawn by John Chen. *Markers and color pencil on Strathmore Bristol paper.* [*Courtesy John Chen.*]

OFFICE OF FOREIGN BUILDINGS OPERATIONS, U.S. DEPARTMENT OF STATE/CABELLERO ARCHITECTS: Lounge Room, U.S. Interest Section, Havana, Cuba. Drawn by John Chen. *Markers and color pencil on Strathmore Bristol paper.* [*Courtesy John Chen.*]

BRYANT ASSOCIATES: Kappa Alpha Psi International Headquarters, Philadelphia, Pennsylvania. Drawn by John Chen. *Markers, color pencil, and alcohol airbrush on tracing paper.* [Courtesy John Chen.]

BRYANT ASSOCIATES/JOHN CHEN: Barney Circle Bridge. Drawn by John Chen. *Markers, color pencil, and airbrush on Strathmore Bristol paper.* [Courtesy *John Chen*.]

BRYANT ASSOCIATES/JOHN CHEN: Barney Circle Bridge. Drawn by John Chen. *Markers, color pencil, and airbrush on Strathmore Bristol paper.* [Courtesy *John Chen.*]

WRIGHT ARCHITECTS: Bangladesh Embassy in Washington, D.C. (competition entry). Drawn by John Chen. *Markers, color pencil, and airbrush on Strathmore Bristol paper.* [*Courtesy John Chen.*]

CSR INTERNATIONAL: China Cinema City and Resort Village, Shenzhen, China. Drawn by John Chen. *Markers, color pencil, and airbrush on Strathmore Bristol paper.* [*Courtesy John Chen.*]

BRYANT ASSOCIATES/JOHN CHEN: United Supreme Council Building, Washington, D.C. Drawn by John Chen. *Markers, color pencil, and alcohol airbrush on tracing paper (clouds erased by electric eraser). [Courtesy John Chen.]*

Pennsylvania Avenue Development Corporation: Federal Bureau of Investigation Building streetscape, Washington, D.C. Drawn by John Chen. *Markers and color pencil on Strathmore Bristol paper.* [*Courtesy John Chen.*]

ARTHUR ERICKSON ARCHITECTS: Pershing Square Station, Los Angeles, California. Drawn by Gene Streett. *Technical pen with markers and airbrush on presentation diazo paper.* [*Courtesy Gene Streett.*]

HARRY WEESE & ASSOCIATES: Springfield/Franconia Station, Northern Virginia. Drawn by Gene Streett. *Technical pen with markers and airbrush on presentation paper.* [Courtesy Gene Streett.]

PAUL MA DESIGNS: Urban resort, Japan. Drawn by Christopher Grubbs. *Color pencil on color xerox images.* [*Courtesy Christopher Grubbs Illustrator.*]

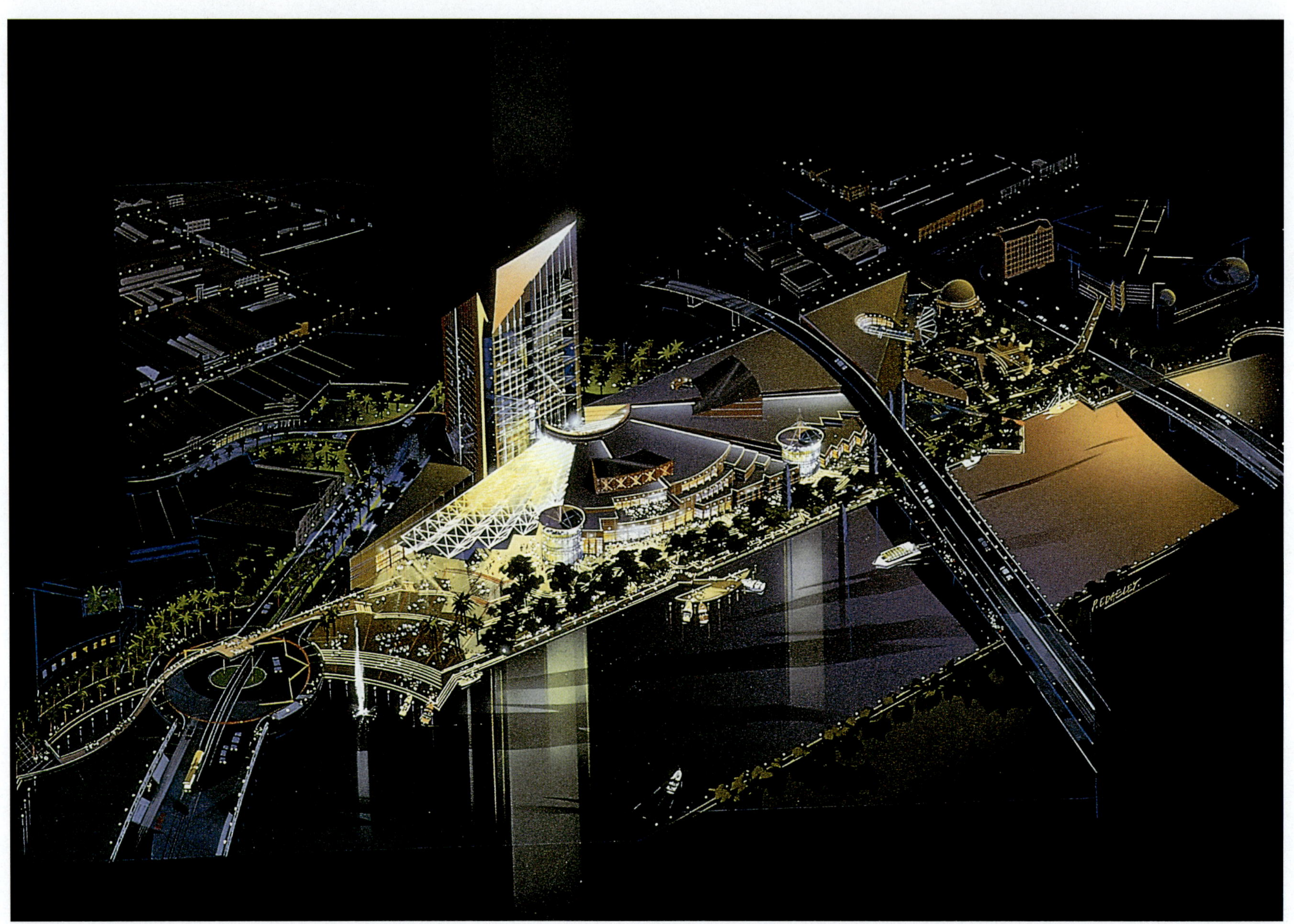

Dale Sprankle, Sprankle Lynd & Sprangue, San Francisco; David Cole Buchan Group, Melbourne, Australia: Melbourne Casino Competition Finalist, Melbourne, Australia. Drawn by Peter Edgeley. *Acrylic airbrush and paint on black board, based on hand drawing setup, model photo, and aerial photography of site.* [*Courtesy Peter Edgeley* (*Australia*).]

DALE SPRANKLE, SPRANKLE LYND & SPRANGUE, SAN FRANCISCO; DAVID COLE BUCHAN GROUP, MELBOURNE, AUSTRALIA: Melbourne Casino Competition Finalist, Melbourne, Australia. Drawn by Peter Edgeley. *Color pencil and overlay paint highlights on heavyweight tracing paper, based on hand setup drawing and site photographs.* [*Courtesy Peter Edgeley (Australia).*]

ANDREW ANDERSONS / PEDDLE THORP ARCHITECTS, SYDNEY, AUSTRALIA: Harbor Apartments, Sydney, Australia. Drawn by Peter Edgeley. *Color pencil and overlay paint highlights on heavyweight tracing paper, based on site photographs and plot from "Design Workshop" running on a Power Mac.* [Courtesy Peter Edgeley (*Australia*).]

PETER EDGELEY ARCHITECT IN ASSOCIATION WITH ANDRAS KELLY LANDSCAPE ARCHITECT/K. BIEDA PROFESSOR OF ARCHITECTURE: Tower Views, Warsaw Square, Warsaw, Poland. Drawn by Peter Edgeley. *Color pencil and overlay paint highlights on heavyweight tracing paper, based on hand setup drawing.* [*Courtesy Peter Edgeley* (*Australia*).]

KEITH GRIFFITHS ARCHITECTS, HONG KONG: Pacific Plaza Atrium, Singapore. Drawn by Peter Edgeley. *Acrylic airbrush and paint on silver gray board, based on hand-set drawing.* [*Courtesy Peter Edgeley* (*Australia*).]

DARYL JACKSON ARCHITECT, MELBOURNE, AUSTRALIA: Segaworld Interior Proposal, Darling Harbor, Sydney, Australia. Drawn by Peter Edgeley. *Montage of photographic cut-outs, acrylic airbrush, and paint on black board, based on a loose, hand drawn setup of a possible interior.* [Courtesy Peter Edgeley (Australia).]

NAVY MARSHALL & GORDON ARCHITECTS: Coast Guard Station, Washington, D.C. Drawn by Richard Fitzhugh. *Watercolor on watercolor board.* [*Courtesy Richard Fitzhugh.*]

ARQUITECTONICA: 42nd Street Redevelopment, Times Square, New York. Drawn by Luis Vanselow. *Watercolor on watercolor board.* [*Courtesy Arquitectonica.*]

Chapter 6

Electronic Drawings in Color

The computer revolution has changed the way we live and the way we work. When first applied to the field of architecture, the computer was used for making construction drawings, restricting itself in the shadow of two-dimensional design. When new three-dimensional programs were available, they were to construct paraline and perspective wireframe—skeleton drawings without solid form and color. The early electronic color programs had very limited colors and took a long time to print.

Since that time, computer-aided design and design communication have increased manyfold in industrial countries as well as developing countries. With the new programs, architects can jump right into three-dimensional design, which enables him / her to visualize his / her project much closer to reality. The computer is not only used for construction drawings, but for the early stages of design, and throughout the whole process of design. Three-dimensional drawings are not just pretty drawings to impress people; they became an integral part of of design and are more frequently used than ever before. The colors available in computer programs range into seven-digit numbers compared to three-digit numbers in conventional media. With its ability to integrate light effects, radiosity, shading, and other elements, the digital drawing can be very close to the reality of the unbuilt environment. The childhood dream of walking into a painting or a movie can be fulfilled by this digital medium which produces video and animation as well as sound effects.

Talking about timesaving and troubleshooting, nothing can be compared to digital drawings. In Chapter 4, "Pen and Ink Drawings with Color," I mentioned that from one pen and ink master print, one can produce a few versions of color drawings. Digital drawings can produce numerous drawings with one effort. It is truly hard to make changes in conventional color renderings. The only way to make these changes is by applying airbrush or cut and paste. All these are not only time-consuming but sometimes displeasing to the eye. Changes made with the computer are a breeze.

Early color digital drawings were very time-consuming and without the necessary entourage—bare drawings with rigid images of structures. Many people worried about the technical look of these drawings. This feud between "tech" and "touch" started at the very early stage of this digital medium. Since that time, many have striven to change this feud to a reconciliation. Nowadays, there are programs that imitate hand-drawn softness, textures, and sensitivity. But behind all this, the human factor is most important. As Mieczylaw Boryslawski has said, "Many architects would argue that the traditional method of hand rendering gives the drawing a human touch, whereas the synthetic rendering tends to look somewhat plastic. This argument has some validity and it takes an experienced person to produce electronic rendering that will satisfy an experienced renderer." He is absolutely correct because no matter how advanced the computer is, it is still a tool. No matter how smart this tool is, it is up to the person who controls the computer. Mr. Boryslawski was a distinguished architect and skilled renderer who has also become a computer artist and he knows all the relationships between "tech" and "touch." Therefore, he can create those photorealistic, yet artistic, images shown in this chapter.

The other approach is the computer / hand composite approach developed by Paul Stevenson Oles, FAIA / Advanced Media Design Inc. While Advanced Media Design Inc. is doing the computer modeling, and having it printed on watercolor paper with an inkjet printer, the renowned architectural perspectivist Paul Stevenson Oles is going over the printout with Prismacolor pencils and giving the drawings a "touchy" look. There may be many other methods which are in the process of developing. Readers should look into these different opportunities and develop their own versions of this "tech" and "touch" combination.

Mario Botta: San Francisco Museum of Modern Art, San Francisco, California. *3-D computer model and rendering by Mieczyslaw Boryslawski, modeled in Turbo 3-D, rendered in Lightscape on IBM PC.* [*Courtesy View By View Inc.*]

RAAD, UESVGI Architects: Proposed office building for Honolulu, Hawaii. *3-D computer model and rendering by France Israel and Claire Schenebeck, Macintosh computer, modeled in Turbo 3-D, rendered with Electric Image.* [*Courtesy View By View Inc.*]

ABOVE: PHOTOGRAPH OF THE MOUNT ZION MEDICAL CENTER

BELOW: DIGITAL RENDERING FROM A COMPUTER MODEL OF THE PROPOSED MOUNT ZION CANCER RESEARCH CENTER

HGA AND ESS ARCHITECTS: University of California at San Francisco, Mount Zion Cancer Center, San Francisco, California. *3-D computer model and rendering by France Israel and Claire Schenebeck, Macintosh computer, modeled in Turbo 3-D, rendered in Electric Image.* [*Courtesy View By View Inc.*]

STANG AND NEWDOW: Istanbul 2000, proposed Olympic Park for the Olympics, Istanbul, Turkey. *3-D computer modeling and rendering by View By View Inc., Macintosh computer, modeled in Turbo 3-D, rendered in Electric Image.* [*Courtesy View By View Inc.*]

PATRI BURLAGE MERKER: Scam Discovery Center, a shopping center, Bangkok, Thailand. *3-D computer model by Tom Harry, PBM, rendering and animation by France Israel, modeled in AutoCAD on IBM PC, rendered and animated in Electric Image.* [*Courtesy View By View Inc.*]

LEARN TECHNOLOGY INTERACTIVE (PRODUCER) TIME WARNER ELECTRONIC PUBLISHING (PUBLISHER): QIN, Tomb of the Middle Kingdom, Geomancy Chamber. An interactive CD-ROM game based on the unexplored archeological site of the first Emperor of China. *3-D computer modeling and rendering by View By View Inc., Macintosh computer, modeled in Form-Z, rendered in Electric Image.* [*Courtesy View By View Inc.*]

LEARN TECHNOLOGY INTERACTIVE (PRODUCER)/TIME WARNER ELECTRONIC PUBLISHING (PUBLISHER): QIN, Tomb of the Middle Kingdom, Geomancy Chamber. An interactive CD-ROM game based on the unexplored archeological site of the first Emperor of China. *3-D computer modeling and rendering by View By View Inc., Macintosh computer, modeled in Form-Z, rendered in Electric Image.* [*Courtesy View By View Inc.*]

THE STUBBINS ASSOCIATES INC.: The Hotel at the World Trade Center, Boston, Massachusetts. All 3-D modeling and rendering: Advanced Media Design Inc. Additional 3D modeling by Chris Leary. *Generated in AutoCAD r.12, imported to 3D Studio r.3, then composite onto the photograph using Hi-Res QFX r.4 and PhotoShop r.2.5.* [Courtesy Advanced Media Design Inc.]

PEI COBB FREED AND PARTNERS: Shanghai Business Center, Shanghai, China. *Computer/hand composite: inkjet print from computer modified by prismacolor on a laser printer on watercolor paper.* [Courtesy Paul Stevenson Oles, FAIA/Advanced Media Design Inc.]

PEI COBB FREED AND PARTNERS: Shanghai Business Center, Shanghai, China. *Computer/hand composite: inkjet print from computer modified by prismacolor on a laser printer on watercolor paper.* [*Courtesy Paul Stevenson Oles, FAIA/Advanced Media Design Inc.*]

PEI COBB FREED AND PARTNERS: Shining Tower/Hotel Complex, Taipei, Taiwan. *Computer/hand composite: inkjet print from computer modified by prismacolor on a laser printer on watercolor paper.* [*Courtesy Paul Stevenson Oles, PSO,FAIA/Advanced Media Design Inc.*]

ELKUS MANFREDI ARCHITECTS (HOWARD ELKUS, FAIA): 128 State Street Renovation, Boston, Massachusetts. Drawn by Advanced Media Design w/Paul Stevenson Oles, FAIA. All 3-D modeling: Advanced Media Design. Original photograph by Peter Vanderwalker. The detail and resolution are a function of the digital process, but the overall unity and tone of the piece are not. [*Courtesy Paul Stevenson Oles, FAIA/Advanced Media Design Inc.*]

KOHN PEDERSEN FOX ASSOCIATES (W. PEDERSEN, FAIA): The Greater Buffalo International Airport, Buffalo, New York. All 3-D modeling and rendering by Advanced Media Design Inc. *Electronic model in AutoCAD r.12, faxing wireframes and mark-ups, created in Animator Pro r.1, PhotoShop r.2.5 or Ron Scott's Hi-Res QFX r.4.* [*Courtesy Advanced Media Design Inc.*]

KOVERT-HAWKINS ARCHITECTS: New Office & Chair Plant, Paoli, Inc., Orleans, Indiana. Drawn by John Hawkins and Susan Biasiolli. *Modeled and rendered on Mac Quadra using Strata StudioPro and Autocad.* [*Courtesy John Hawkins.*]

KOVERT-HAWKINS ARCHITECTS: New Office & Chair Plant, Paoli, Inc., Orleans, Indiana. Drawn by John Hawkins. *Modeled and rendered on Mac Quadra using Strata StudioPro and Autocad.* [*Courtesy John Hawkins.*]

PERKINS & WILL ARCHITECTS: Airport Competition, Seoul, Korea. Drawn by John Hawkins. *Modeled and rendered on Mac Quadra using Strata StudioPro and Autocad.* [*Courtesy John Hawkins and Rael Slutsky.*]

PERKINS & WILL ARCHITECTS: Airport Competition, Seoul, Korea. Drawn by John Hawkins. *Modeled and rendered on Mac Quadra using Strata Version3d.* [*Courtesy John Hawkins and Rael Slutsky.*]

HLW INTERNATIONAL LLP: Corporate entrance of a speculative office building, Shanghai, China. Drawn by Thomas Singer. *Computer rendering on Intergraph 600 workstation; software is Intergraph Modelview, Bently Microstation, Adobe Photoshop.* [© HLW International LLP 1996.]

HLW INTERNATIONAL LLP: Proposal for a lobby view, New Haven, Connecticut. Drawn by Thomas Singer. *Computer rendering on Intergraph 600 workstation; software is Intergraph Modelview, Bently Microstation, Adobe Photoshop.* [© HLW International LLP 1996.]

HOWARD ASSOCIATES: The Super House (one of the views from a computer animation). Location unidentified. Drawn by Edward Howard. This drawing is selected from one of the first computer rendering series ever executed. *Wireframe on Autocad 3-D, rendering on Wavefront.* [*Courtesy Howard Associates.*]

Taiwan University Arena, Taipei, Taiwan. Drawn by Thunder Image Inc. [*Courtesy Haigo Shen & Associates, Architects and Engineers* (*Taiwan*).]

Kaohsiung Arena Competition entry. A study on membrane and steel structure for the 25,000-seat arena, Kaohsiung, Taiwan. Drawn by Buo-Yuan Hsu. *Built and rendered with AutoCad and 3-D Studio on PC.* [*Courtesy Haigo Shen & Associates, Architects and Engineers* (*Taiwan*).]

Taichung New Civic Center Competition entry, City Government, Taichung, Taiwan. Drawn by Eddie Young. *Built and rendered with AutoCad and 3-D Studio on PC.* [*Courtesy Haigo Shen & Associates, Architects and Engineers* (*Taiwan*).]

Fan De Office HQ, competition winning entry, Taipei, Taiwan. Drawn by Eddie Young. *Built and rendered with AutoCad and 3-D Studio on PC.* [*Courtesy Haigo Shen & Associates, Architects and Engineers* (*Taiwan*).]

Taichung Post Office HQ, Computer Backup Center Competition entry, Taichung, Taiwan. Drawn by Eddie Young. *Built and rendered with AutoCad and 3-D Studio on PC.* [*Courtesy Haigo Shen & Associates, Architects and Engineers* (*Taiwan*).]

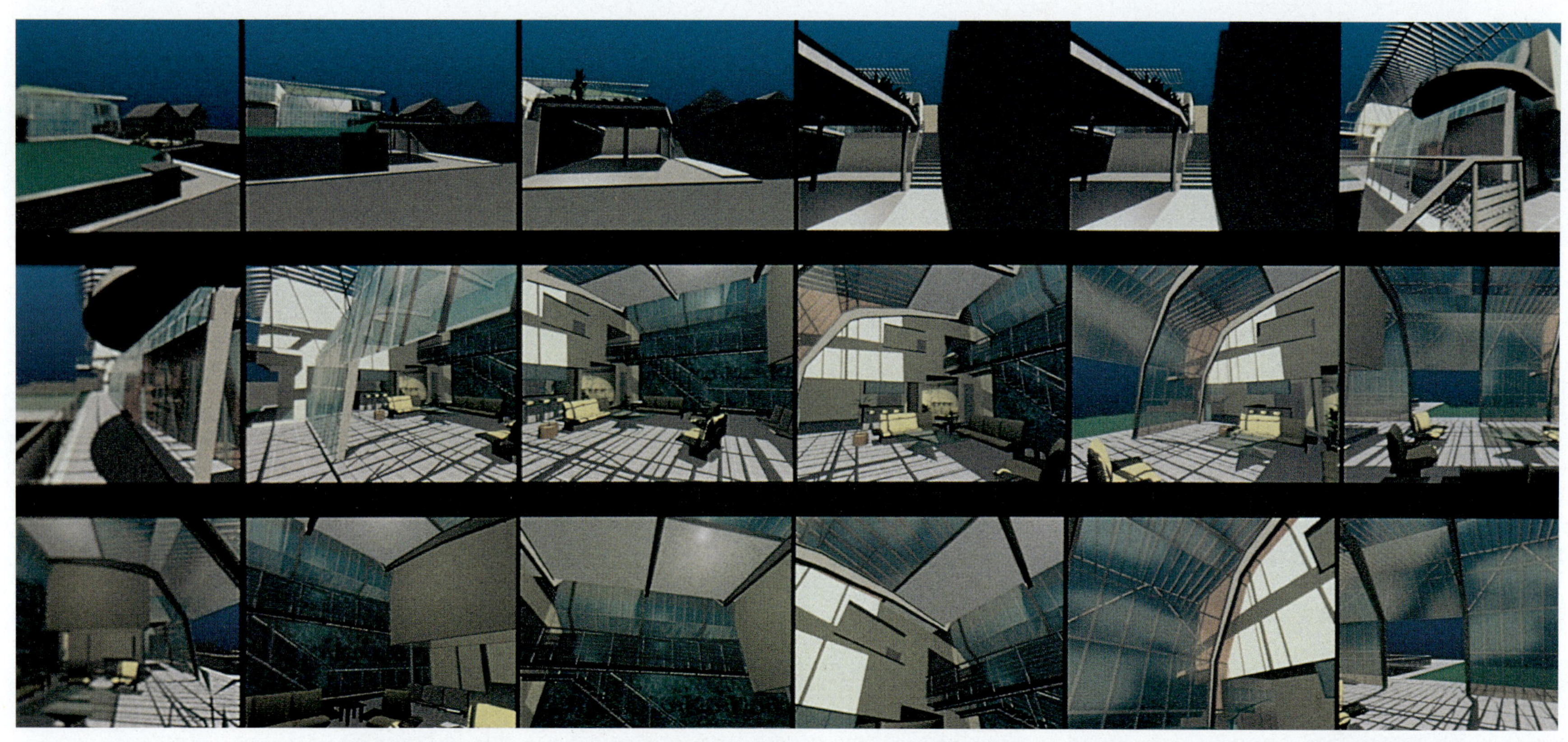

T. R. HAMZAH & YEANG SDN. BHD: Soon House, Penang, Malaysia. Drawn by Ken Yeang. *3-D Studio, later downloaded onto video format for fly-throughs on VHS video presentations.* [*Courtesy Ken Yeang* (*Malaysia*).]

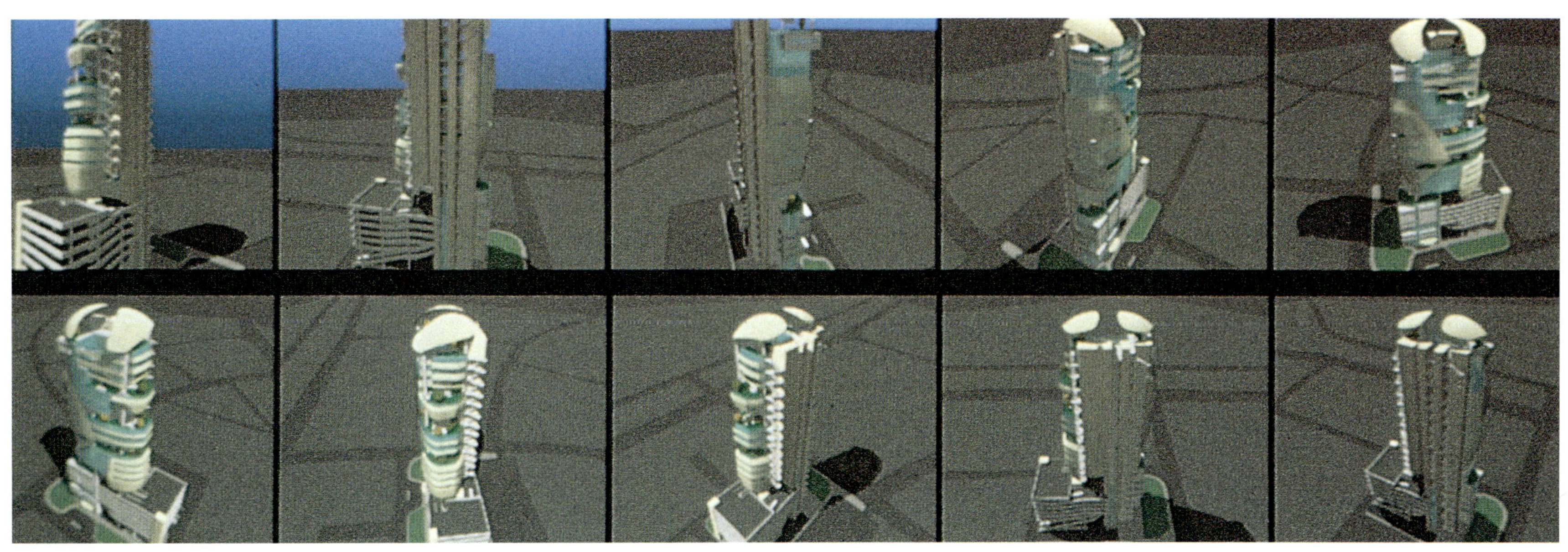

T. R. HAMZAH & YEANG SDN. BHD: Hitechniaga Tower, Kuala Lumpur, Malaysia. Drawn by Ken Yeang. *3-D Studio, later downloaded onto video format for fly-throughs on VHS video presentations.* [*Courtesy Ken Yeang* (*Malaysia*).]

ABOUT THE AUTHOR

John S. M. Chen, AIA, is an associate professor in the School of Architecture and Planning at Howard University. He is also a registered architect with over 30 years of professional experience domestically and internationally, having designed many commercial, institutional, transportational, educational, residential, and health-related projects. He is the author of *Architecture in Pen and Ink* and *Architectural Perspective Grids: Three-Dimensional Design and Perspective Construction Simplified*, with coauthor William T. Cooper, AIA.